"One Veteran's Journey"

"To Heal the Wounds of War"
"Revised"

By Jack Gutman

ISBN 978-0692-64872-8

ISBN   10 0692648720

DEDICATION

To my family.
They make the journey worthwhile.

ACKNOWLEDGMENTS

I want to take this opportunity to thank the many people that have touched and made my life a blessed one. First, I want to thank my wonderful wife of sixty-eight years, who has been so patient with me through all our married life. I am so glad you stuck it out. By the way Jo, "I love you, I love you!" Those "I love you's" are part of a private game she and I play daily. The way it works is that after 12 o'clock p.m. each day, we touch each other and say, "I love you." It's a win-win situation for both of us.

To my children, Lesley, Paula, and Craig, I want to thank you for the wonderful contributions of hope and happiness you've brought into my life. Each of you has made a significant impact on my life by your words and actions, touching my life in so many precious ways. I could never ask for more and I am so proud of each one of you. Craig, the days we worked together in the wallpapering field were bonding times I will never forget. Lesley, your prayers and all the help you gave me in helping me write my first book, and this one has taught your father a great lesson (your children can get a lot smarter than you). Paula, you have given me many good ideas on various things in life. The expansion of this book is one example.

There have been many friends and relatives who have always been there for me with love, wisdom, and at times financial support. I've personally thanked them all, but I want to acknowledge some of them herein as well. To my brother Mel, and his wife Mary, who were always there with wisdom and often financial support, I say "Thanks." Chuck Pennington and his wife, Socorrin, have also blessed Jo and me in many ways. When things looked bleak, you both were there with love and financial support. You are great examples of Christians doing God's work. Thank you!

Thanks to my dear friend Steve Gonzalez for your wonderful friendship and financial help. We have shared many laughs and tears, and I could not ask for a better friend.

To my friend George, who is a man of God and has also blessed my life in many ways; how can I ever forget the kindness and love shown through prayer, fellowship, and the many financial blessings you have provided? You bought me my first video camera to start my small business called "Memoirs of Your Life" (this is where I make videos of people's lives to leave for their loved ones after they have departed). Thanks so much for your love and support.

To my sister Jeanette and her son Don Tirado, who helped us with love and finances, I express my gratitude for your generosity. You have such big hearts. You played a part in teaching me the importance of touching lives and making that lifestyle a priority in my own life. To Patrick, Chris, Jenna, Erin, and Casey, you have made me very proud with all your accomplishments, and the men and women of character you've all turned out to be. Erin, can't thank you enough for your ideas on how to make my book better. Thanks for the hard work.

To my other sister Barbara and my late sister Micky, your advice and love meant so much to me. To my late brothers, Walter, Martin, and Mitch, who always provided me with new jokes, I express my gratitude. Thank you, Mitch, for the blessings you gave me with your love. When things were rough, you were always there. How I remember those wonderful dinners we had together. Mitch's daughter Lisa Gutman, a successful realtor, was a lifesaver when she helped me get a new Hyundai Elantra. I will never forget you, Lisa.

To my nieces, Carol Stacy and Naomi Grier, you were always gracious with your love and always laughed at my jokes. To Dave, Naomi's other half, thank you for your kindness and love you have extended to me. To my nephews, Gabe Jr. and Sanford Tirado, you both have given me many happy days. To my late brother-in-law, Gabe Tirado, I will always remember the many good times we had growing up together. I will see you someday in the future. We may get an opportunity to sail again in a new unique way. To my niece, Robbie McDonnell, and her husband, Mike, along with their two children, Josh and Danielle, as a family, you know what it means to have trials and tribulations, yet you trusted God to pull you through. You're an inspiration.

Great thanks to my therapist, Dylan Bender, for giving me new hope for living and helping me to get rid of the terrible pain related to Post Traumatic Stress Disorder. I can now talk about it and use what I experienced to help others. I could not have done it without you.

A special thanks to Congresswoman Loretta Sanchez and Ms. Laura Martinez for going to bat for me with the Veterans' Administration when I needed help. Your efforts have given my wife and me a promising future filled with hope. I will never forget you. I know you both are so busy with many other matters, yet you took the time to help a veteran who was in a desperate situation. Again, thanks so much! Thank you to the Veterans' Administration for your tireless efforts to expedite my pension.

Also, deep gratitude goes to my wonderful church, Eastside Christian Church, for not only blessing me with spiritual gifts, but also for providing financial help to my wife and me when we were in great need. Your compassion towards us and so many other people is exactly what God teaches us to do. Sandy Printer came into my life in Toastmasters, and mentored me in so many ways. I personally thank you for encouraging me to finally get on the ball to write this book.

There are many other people that have blessed my life. Though I was unable to individually address you, God knows who you are and will bless you.

INTRODUCTION

What were you doing when you were eighteen? Cruising the main drag of your town? Hanging out at the beach with friends? Grabbing a burger with your buddies? That's what most eighteen year olds I knew were doing, but not me. I was in uniform on an APA troop ship about to land on the beach in Normandy. It was June 6, 1944, and my head was filled with a combination of the pride I felt in serving my country, and the greatest feeling of terror I'd ever known.

I could see the ships shelling the beach, hear the explosions of bombs dropping from planes and see men dying by the hundreds. Over eight thousand in all would die that day. The landing boats were about to drop us into deep water with heavy packs on our backs. A treacherous situation, but it was the best they could do because of steel girders and land mines designed to prevent them from landing on the sand. If you've ever watched a war movie, you might have a slight understanding of what I'm talking about, but let me tell you, the real thing is far worse than you could ever imagine.

With my heavy pack on my back, I somehow made it out of the deep water, stepped on to the beach and

1

started looking for my wounded comrades. My job was to patch them up and evacuate them. Sounds simple enough, but all of my training didn't come close to preparing me for what I felt when I saw the first wounded soldier. He was shot in the leg near the groin. There was a lot of blood and he was screaming in agony. He wasn't much older than I was, and his life was in my hands. I remember how terrified I was and how part of my mind just wanted to escape and not let the true horror of the scene in front of me into my brain. But I was a trained soldier in the United States Navy, and I had a huge job to do. There was no choice, no turning back.

After that moment, my mind went into a survival autopilot of sorts. I was running on pure adrenaline and instinct, not thought. There was so much happening around me, that even now, seventy years later, I can't begin to recall it all. Most of what sticks out in my mind are the most visceral memories. The sounds of explosions, men screaming for their mothers, land mines, machine guns spitting out one hundred and fifty bullets a minute, mowing down my comrades before they could even get to the beach. The loud sound of my own heartbeat pounding in my ears as I tried my best to patch up wounds fast and move on to the next man. The visions of blood on the sand, barbed wire everywhere, hundreds of uniformed men lying on the ground squirming in agony, some of them dying in my arms as I told them they would be alright, still remains in my mind today.

Meanwhile, back on the home front, my best friends were likely out with their girlfriends enjoying a beautiful June day. Maybe laughing over fries and a burger at our favorite spot, catching a show, or spending the afternoon cutting grass for a neighbor, while I was doing everything I could to stay alive. I made it through that day and the war alive, and when I returned home a hero (although I didn't think of myself as one) with five medals for my contribution in the European Theatre, Normandy, Pacific Theatre, Okinawa Invasion, and the occupation of Japan, I thought I was alright, that I had escaped unscathed. But as time went on, I came to realize that while I had returned home uninjured, World War II left permanent scars and wounds on me that I wouldn't fully comprehend until many years later.

FROM THE BEGINNING

In 1925, Calvin Coolidge was president, the Pittsburgh Pirates won the World Series, F. Scott Fitzgerald published *The Great Gatsby*, and I was born in San Francisco, California. Meanwhile, thousands of miles away in Munich, Germany, a young activist named Adolf Hitler resurrected the Nationalsozialistische Deutsche Arbeiterpartei political party (NSDAP), otherwise known as The Nazi Party.

I was the third of what would end up being nine children. My father Louis was an American who fought in the US Army in World War I. My mother Gertrude was a Russian aristocrat whose family fled the country when the Bolshevik regime took over in 1917. My parents met at the Grand Hotel in Shanghai, China, where my father was working as a concierge after the war. By my grandfather's standards, Louis was a commoner and not a suitable partner for his daughter, but my father was smart, charming, and spoke many languages, and my mother fell head over heels for him.

My parents were married soon after meeting, and my father brought her to America. Like many young American families living in the 1920's, we struggled to put bread on the table. When the Great Depression hit in

1929, times became even harder for our family. My father sold apples on the street just so he could buy food for us to eat. Having children of my own now, I cannot imagine the frustration my parents must have felt during this time, but their deep love for one another seemed to get them through.

I was four years old on Black Friday, too young to understand what was going on. By 1929, my parents had five children: Ralph, Jeanette, myself, Micky, and Mel. We lived in a small apartment with one bathroom. I grew up believing that God lived in our bathroom because my father used to pound on the door and yell, "GOD, ARE YOU STILL IN THERE?"

My mother found a healthy, inexpensive way to feed us. She made a bulgur wheat dish called Kasha. We had it for breakfast with sugar and milk, for lunch cooked with some vegetables, and dinner made with other types of vegetables. We very seldom saw meat on the table because it was too expensive in those days. One thing was for sure: what we ate was nourishing, although as children we didn't feel that way about it at the time. Most parents tell their children to eat their vegetables. For our family, if you didn't eat your vegetables, you'd literally starve. How's that for ironic?

My parents were loving but strict, and as was common during that time, if we did anything wrong we got my father's belt. My father worked as a traveling salesmen at that time, so our family moved a lot. By the time I was fourteen we had lived in San Francisco, Minneapolis, Detroit, Washington D.C., and ended up in New York City. My brothers Martin, Mitch, Walter, and my sister Barbara were born during those years. That gave us a family of nine children.

Games and entertainment were of our own making. We used cupcake tins with numbers in it and used a ping pong ball that we bounced into the tin tray to try to get the highest score. The toilet paper roll was my horn, which I called my toot-to-toot. Outside there was Stickball, (we used a rubber ball and the handle of a broomstick). You bounced the ball and tried to hit it and we made bases to touch as we ran around them. It was lots of fun.

Things had to be organized to keep a big household like ours running properly. For daily chores, my father made a list of twelve things to be done, and we would each choose one item from the list to do. However, you could not do the same chore again for another three days. He tried to make a game out of it. At first we tried to do the easy chores and eventually we learned to do the worst chores first, such as cleaning the bathroom or mopping the floors, to get them out of the way. My father and mother somehow got us to do these chores daily with no complaints. Smart parents.

My father had a tangible whistle that commanded immediate attention. When he leaned out of the window, put his lips together and whistled that familiar sound that we all knew, we came home right away. There were no acceptable excuses. If we did not comply, the belt was waiting. Consequently, no one was ever late more than once. It was important to come home immediately because our family always had dinner together. There were no exceptions.

When my father told jokes or was talking, no one interrupted him. If you did, you got a look from him that made it clear you were treading on thin ice and you better shape up. Still, in spite of all of his rules, my father was a warm and kind man, who worked hard to provide for his family and was loved us all.

My mom and dad were both Godly people, my mother from a traditional Russian Orthodox family and my father from the Jewish faith. Therefore, we grew up hearing about prayer and trusting God on a daily basis.

Though we did not go to any church, we believed that God would take care of all our needs. Occasionally, there were times when doubt would come into our minds, and we wondered if we were indeed being looked after.

One Christmas, when I was fourteen, the family was having a particularly tough year in New York. We had little food in our home and absolutely no possibility of Christmas presents. My father went down to the corner to get a free Christmas tree on Christmas Eve so that we could have a bit of holiday cheer. We felt sad and disappointed that we weren't going to have a real Christmas, but as always, there was contentment in being together with our family.

My father returned with the tree and we did our best to decorate it with hand-made decorations we created with things we had around the house. After a little while, we heard a knock at the door. We opened it to find a well-dressed lady with her chauffer standing there. They had bags of food, including a big turkey. We had not had meat of any kind in the house for many days. This kind-hearted woman also had gifts of toys for all of us children, as well as helpful things my parent could use. I thought I had died and gone to heaven, I was so excited!

We found out that a few days before, my younger brother Martin, was at a local toy store looking in the window. This same woman walked up to him and said, "I'll bet you're going to get lots of presents for Christmas." Martin had told her that we were poor and that we were not getting anything for Christmas. She made it her mission to find out where we lived and how many boys and girls were in the family. I have no idea what her name was, but that kind and generous woman was like an angel sent directly from God. It's been over seventy-four years, and I still see that Christmas Eve so vividly in my mind. It was one of the best Christmases we ever had!

Many years later, as an adult, I took my own children and did something similar for a poor family that I knew of. I was so touched to see my two daughters and son give their favorite toys as gifts to this poor family. My daughters gave beautiful dolls to the girls in that family; and my son gave an expensive, almost new robot that I had bought him, to the boy in that poor family. The look on that boy's face when he received that robot as a gift was priceless. It made all the sacrifice worthwhile.

Jack's Mom and Dad

Our Wedding Day June 22, 1947

GROWING UP

By 1940, I was sixteen years old and a teenager living in New York City. In those days, I felt like I needed to learn to survive. In my mind, surviving meant I had to join a gang, because they provided protection and camaraderie. Meanwhile, in Europe British soldiers not much older than I had died defending France from Hitler's Nazi Army.

The same year I joined the gang called The Panthers, the British Army evacuated the beaches of Dunkirk and Winston Churchill declared that Great Britain would never surrender to the Axis Powers. Little did I know that the United States had ceased trade with Japan, cutting off 90 percent of their oil supply, which would ultimately lead to the Pearl Harbor attack. In four short years I would find myself on a different French beach fighting in the exact same war.

Being a Panther began as a positive experience. Getting my very own silver Panther jacket was a huge deal. It made me feel proud and important. In many ways I think it was my very first experience feeling the pride of a uniform. We were a proud gang and wore the jackets everywhere.

School proved to be tougher as more than one gang

from our neighborhood attended our school. We had many fights with other gangs. Sometimes fights were just one guy from our gang fighting someone from the other gang. At other times it was everyone for themselves. We mainly used fists, but occasionally someone would use a knife. That usually happened when things got intensely serious and anger turned to rage. Unlike the gang violence we see today, guns were not used because of the Sullivan Law that existed in New York in those days. If you carried a gun and they found it on you, you were sent to prison for ten years.

We were young, careless, and did crazy things like hanging onto the back of a bus and taking a dangerous ride downtown. We also had BB gun fights on the rooftops, and we were even so careless as to leap from roof to roof, jumping over a six-foot gap. All of the fun came to an end when we lost a great friend named Joey, who lost his footing and fell six stories to his death.

The second uniform I donned in those days was the one that helped pull me out of the gang life and steer me in the right direction. A local church minister came by my house and told us about his church. My parents, being religious people, were interested in what he had to say. The church had a Drum and Bugle Corps there. However, if you wanted to be in the band, then you had to go to a Sunday school class. To have a nice band uniform as well as learn to play drums and a bugle intrigued me, so I joined the Sunday school class and the band. I really enjoyed playing those instruments, and my father, being a former military man, was proud.

At this time, I did not know God in a personal way or have a relationship with him. The Sunday school class and band experience was my first introduction to God prior to going into the service. My life later changed because of my experiences and growth with God. I would like to caution you young people to remember that although you are young, you do not have a guarantee on how many years you have on this earth. I have seen too many of my buddies that had big dreams of their future, only to see their dead bodies on some beach or ship a few days later. I was given a second chance of going through a war and two invasions before finding out how important it is having something bigger than me to hold on to.

HERE COMES THE NAVY

On December 7, 1941, the Japanese military bombed our Naval base at Pearl Harbor. I remember feeling enraged and shocked when I heard the news. I never dreamed that a small country like Japan would ever do that to the United States. Yet in their surprise attack, they caused so much death and damage to our fleet that America finally joined the war effort.

Maybe it was my history of gang fighting, maybe I was inspired by playing in a military style band at church, but I was angry and wanted to fight. My father would not sign for me to join the military, as I was just a few weeks shy of seventeen. The following September, with America in the thick of World War II, I finally talked my parents into letting me join the Navy.

I assured them that I would have three meals a day and sleep in a nice bed. After they signed the papers for me, I went down to the Navy recruiter's office to join. I remember feeling exhilarated that I would be fighting for my country to defend freedom. I walked into the recruiter's office, and discovered that they had two lines, one for four years in the Navy and one for the duration of the war. I chose the duration of the war line because I figured I would take a chance that the war would be shorter than four years. While my original intention was to stick it out and fight until the war was over, it ended up being a good choice because the war ended two and a half years later.

Just a few short weeks later I said goodbye to my parents and siblings and traveled to boot camp in Long Island, New York. I remember the train ride there, feeling exhilarated that I was going to make a difference in the war effort. I had no idea then what was in store for me.

Military life was completely a whole new way of living. I went into the service a cocky kid from New York with a "wise guy" mindset and an attitude of wanting to do things my way. I learned pretty quickly that I was not running the show and that when my drill sergeant yelled, "Jump," my response would always be "How high, sir?" I also learned to appreciate my mother. The years of her washing and pressing my clothes had come to an end. In the service, I learned to take care of my own belongings and I became begrudgingly self-sufficient nearly overnight.

After boot camp, I took tests for special training. I was most interested in being an aerial radioman and learn radio operations because it seemed to have lots of action, so I took the test for it and passed. There were also options to learn to be a machine gunner on the plane.

In the Pacific, medics were getting killed by the Japanese the minute they hit the beach, due to the fact that they wore helmets that had a big red cross on them that made them easily spotted targets. According to the Geneva Convention the enemy was not allowed to shoot at the medics, but that rule was ignored by the Japanese. Their thinking was that if you killed the medics, you killed the morale of the fighting men.

Consequently, with the loss of so many killed in prior

battles, they needed to train replacements for our mission and I was drafted out of the lot. When they informed me of my change in duties, I felt a similar feeling of pride and terror. I find it ironic now that someone like me who couldn't stand the sight of blood, even in the gang fights, would end up a medic, but because of the shortage in the Navy, I didn't have a choice. Looking back, I believe God was watching over me as many aerial gunners were killed.

I was sent to Bainbridge Medical School for a six-month accelerated training course in assisting during surgery and battlefield treatments of all kinds. Though it was actually a one-year course, it was shortened to six months by the trainees putting in a lot of time and effort. We went to medical school from eight in the morning to noon. Then we took a one-hour lunch break, and back to school until five o'clock in the evening. After we had a dinner break, it was back to school from seven until nine o'clock at night. Only after that was there any free time. Sundays were our relaxing time, once we got through with any studying. After medical school we were sent home for two weeks of leave before going to Europe. It was truly emotional and wonderful to be back with my family and I remember being sad when it was time to deploy.

I was sent to Europe on a big British ship called the Aquitania with all the other men that trained with me. We were at sea for many days sailing to England. It was the first time I'd ever left the country. We were sent to Ireland and Scotland to pick up supplies and nurses. At first it was very exciting seeing these new countries and meeting new people, but we soon began to understand the severity of the situation when we got to Netley, England.

The hospital there was very large. It had not been taken care of for some time and we had to clean it from

14

top to bottom. It took over four months to get this giant hospital ready. Our medical force consisted of about two thousand people, and none of us had any idea what was coming. We later came to find out we had been working in preparation for the invasion of Normandy.

On the weekends, half of the force could get some time off to relax and enjoy England. During that leave, I tried to enjoy life the way most eighteen-year-olds would. I went with my new friends and comrades to the towns of Netley and South Hampton, but we soon came to see that there wasn't much left of the towns. There were many bombed-out homes and buildings destroyed by the Germans.

The Germans developed a new rocket bomb called the Buzz Bomb. When they flew over, you could hear the buzz sound it made. When the buzz stopped, it came down at an angle hitting the house or building, bringing destruction. Those at the hospital were now vulnerable targets. The buzz bombs came over every day and night.

I remember one particular night that we experienced a very terrifying bombing raid. A few bombs fell near the hospital and we ran to duck under tables to keep debris from falling on us. My friend, Sullivan, who we called Sully, got down on his knees and prayed out loud, "Lord, if it's my time, I am ready." It was the first time I ever gave any thought to actually dying. I had five shipmates that soon became my close buddies. We shared many serious times and many laughs, and we were always there for each other. You have many friends in the service. Although they have all passed on now, the ones you remember are the ones that shared the good times and bad.

As General Eisenhower was preparing for the Normandy Invasion, I was chosen to go into special training with another group of men from the hospital. We were told about the covert plans to attack in

Normandy called Operation Overlord, and we were all sworn to secrecy and kept in a separate section. The outcome of the war rested on the success of this operation, and we all felt the tension.

We didn't know that the U.S. and British armies were working hard at a deception to lead the Germans to believe that we would invade in The Pas de Calais, where the English Channel is smallest. To gain the required air superiority needed to ensure a successful invasion, the Allies launched a bombing campaign which was called Operation Point Blank. Targeting German aircraft production, fuel supplies, airfields, communications infrastructure, and road and rail links were bombed to cut off the north of France and make it more difficult for the Germans to bring up reinforcements. These attacks were also performed all over northern coastal France to avoid revealing the exact location of the upcoming D-Day invasion.

In addition to this, a series of elaborate deceptions code-named Operation Bodyguard were put into effect to prevent the Germans from determining the timing and location of the invasion. The Allies sent a series of fake radio transmissions out to France about the size of the army, and the location, date, and time of the attack. By the time we were ready to invade, the Germans had no idea we were coming.

While in our secret section, we were taught evacuation techniques and prepared for the invasion. On June 6th, 1944 around six a.m., an armada of 5,000 thousand ships, 4,000 landing crafts, 11,000 planes, and 135,000 military men arrived into the very choppy waters of Normandy, France. The night before the invasion, the Navy, wanting to treat the invading forces to a great meal, gave the soldiers whatever they wanted. Unfortunately, many men ate too much and were very seasick before the invasion started. This caused them to make many mistakes due to their condition. One example was leaping off the sides of the landing crafts into deep water with full packs on the back. Many of them could not get the packs off in time and drowned.

Finally, it was my turn and we boarded the boats and waited to invade. The weather in the English Channel was not good; there were threats of storms and the Allies debated heavily whether or not we'd invade now or wait. I'll never forget the feeling of agony waiting to invade.

My unit was in the fourteenth wave to invade Utah Beach. It was not as bad as Omaha Beach, where we lost thousands of men, but it was a horrible situation nonetheless. The Germans had an uphill advantage. The plan was that the United States Air Force would fly over the German bunkers and drop their bombs, disabling the installations (guns, cannons) and making it easier for the landing invasion. Unfortunately, the pilots missed their targets due to the dense cloud cover. They tried to time the bomb drops, but most of the bombs fell on the other side of the German bunkers. This gave the Germans an advantage to use their powerful machine guns that shot one hundred and fifty bullets a minute, which meant they could slaughter dozens of soldiers in half the time. The men coming off the small boats were killed before they could get a shot off.

When I saw the bombs hitting the beach I thought no one would be alive on shore once our troops landed. There were many men drowning in the water because of heavy equipment when their boats were hit and overturned. The other problem that caused so many deaths were the thousands of land mines that the Germans planted on the beach. Allied tanks were supposed to eliminate a lot of the mines and barbwire; however, many tanks were destroyed by the Germans. Because of German beach barricades, we used special rubber boats that were carrying the tanks closer, but due to rough waters all of them sunk. If the tanks and the Air Force bombing would have gone as planned, many lives could have been saved. The Allied Forces that participated in invasions on the other beaches also took on many casualties. I still see those awful images in my mind today.

It was horrible seeing young men dying all around me. When you are a medic, it becomes very personal to you. Your job is to save lives, and watching those lives stripped away more quickly than you can repair wounds leaves you feeling helpless and frustrated. When you are trying to patch up their wounds knowing they will not survive, it's a terrible feeling.

Even when we knew the men would not make it, we reassured them that they were going to be okay. I heard these young men, who were my age, crying for their mothers as they died in my arms. It breaks my heart even now, thinking back. At that young age, I did not really have a relationship with God, but I found myself praying for the dying men, even though it was something I was never trained for.

Out of 135,000 men that participated in that battle, by evening there were 9,000 American, British, and Canadian men dead. In addition, the men that flew the bombing raids into France and Germany were amazing in their support for us on the beach but their losses were huge as well. They not only lost airplanes, but lost an average of 700 men a day.

After the beach was secure, I was transported back to England and took care of the many wounded in our hospital. I was assigned to the officers' quarters, and I began working to help save as many wounded soldiers as I could. The wounds we treated varied from amputees to shrapnel wounds.

I had one patient that I became close with who was a

young officer. He was married with one child and wanted nothing more than to make it home to his family. Unfortunately, he was losing spinal fluid daily and the doctor told me that he would not make it. I could not bring myself to tell him that he was going to die, and it broke my heart. So instead, I tried to encourage him and I lied about his recovery. He went into a delirious state and then died a few days later. When a person dies on your watch, you have to pack every cavity in his body with cotton to keep him from leaking. This was so traumatic for a man who just turned eighteen years of age. Even now when I think back, I cannot help but wipe away tears.

After the Normandy Invasion and taking care of the wounded in England, I was sent back to New York for a thirty-day leave. I thought that I would get some stateside duty since I had been overseas, but I soon found out that they had other plans for me.

My experiences had changed my outlook on my life and the world. I went into the war with a fervor to fight for my country and protect our freedom, but the experience had been nothing like what I thought when I signed up to join the Navy. Back at home, I thought constantly of the men that had died overseas. I wondered how and why I survived? There I was, a young teenager thrown into a crazy war with thousands of young men like myself dying in front of me. I never dreamed it would be that awful, and that those horrifying images would stick with me now that I was safely at home, and for years to come. Those men would never enjoy family, marriage, and the various joys of life.

I visited the World War II Museum in New Orleans this past September, 2015. I was interviewed by video for 90 minutes and they asked a lot of questions about my experiences and memories. After the interview, I was told, "You are a hero!" My response was "Anyone that fights, brings food and ammunition, plus the support groups like Airman, ships, medics, and the planners are all heroes. We are a team! That is why we strive to win, as a team." The great Commanders and Generals that make the decisions will always be remembered but as a team is how we survived the war.

Normandy Invasion June 6, 1944

Batleship New Mexico Hit By Kamakasi Plane

DO I NEED MORE ACTION?

As my journey as a Navy Medic continued, I was attached to an outfit called the Beach Battalion in California. Our job was to train to accompany the Army and Marine Corps on the beach. My group served as the medical group for the Marines. We were stationed at Camp Pendleton in Oceanside, California. At that time, Highway 101 was just a two-way road going either north to Los Angeles or south to San Diego. The Marine base was on the other side of the road and is still there today.

While in training I observed how tough the training is for the Marines. My first day while training with them, I became so exhausted I passed out and ended up in the hospital. We learned how to go down nets with a full pack and rifle or medical kit from a large ship to the small boats that they used for hitting the beaches. They also used Landing Ship Tanks (LST) for tanks and large cargo, which helped carry the large items and landing troops directly to shore. Though the action was similar to what I experienced in Normandy, it was much more intense. In one case, we were practicing going down the nets along side of the big ship into the small boats, and the man below me slipped and fell into the water. His medical pack was so heavy that he went straight down and drowned. It was such a tragedy to lose someone in a practice drill.

After a few months of training on beach landings, we were assigned to an APA (Attack Personnel Assault) ship. The name of the ship was the USS *Cullman*. This ship carried large personnel plus a lot of small boats. When we boarded the ship headed to Pearl Harbor in Hawaii, we all wondered what was in store for us. I was nervous and apprehensive about what I would face next, and the horrible things I'd seen in Normandy still haunted my thoughts.

When we arrived in Hawaii, we started many practice invasions. We would climb down the nets, go in the small boats and hit the local secluded beaches. During one of our practice drills, we landed on a beach and were secured for the day. A couple of men in our unit had dug into the sand to make a foxhole to sleep in, but these poor men didn't realize they had made their foxhole too close to the road where tanks and armored cars drove on. They lost their lives when a tank ran over them while they were sleeping. We were called to the site of the accident and the sight was something I can't even put into words. Again, two men died in a practice drill and I just couldn't comprehend this senseless loss of life. I understood dying in real action, but how could so much peril be found even in practicing for an invasion?

After weeks of practice we headed out to sea. First we went to the Philippines to pick up supplies and then we went to an island where we could swim and relax. The water was very clear and beautiful. I finally felt myself relax and the pain of what I had experienced was fading, when I got orders along with a few hundred other men to be transferred to another APA called the USS *Bowie*.

The *Bowie* had picked up a large amount of soldiers in Pearl Harbor and, while we had the feeling something was about to begin, we were still kept in the dark by our superiors. Even while I faced the fear of being killed in battle, I began to use humor to cope with my fears and insecurities. I started to tell jokes to my shipmates, using many accents and impressions that, for whatever reason, came naturally to me. I could do a Jewish dialect as well as French, Russian, Italian, American Southern accents, and a few others. When I got the laughs, it built up my low self-esteem and pretty soon I had a bunch of sailors and Army men listening to my jokes and laughing. Joke-telling was a way for me to gain acceptance and approval, plus it was a diversion from the wounds of war. Joke-telling in the service was the start of what was to become my future line of work.

The ship spent many days at sea, and pretty soon we joined a whole fleet of ships of all types. We even had Navy destroyers protecting our ship, which had many Army men aboard. Soon we were told that we would be part of a big operation that could change the outcome of the war. We were going to invade Okinawa, a very big stronghold of Japan. Controlling Okinawa was crucial so that we could use the airfields and the island for the future invasion of Japan.

We were also told that the Japanese were very tough fighters. They had never lost a war. They would fight to the death and not surrender like soldiers from other countries did. That idea hit me like asking General Custer if he would like more Indians. My odds of survival were looking more and more bleak.

We arrived in Okinawa in the pitch black of night. The water was still and everything around us felt eerily calm, but at daybreak all hell broke loose. The invasion began with thousands of Marines and soldiers attacking all areas of Okinawa. There wasn't a lot of gunfire on the beaches, as most of the gunfire was inland where the heart of the battle began.

We received the casualties on the beaches from the

battles, as our area was safer. The sights were horrible. I could hear the agony of those young men begging to be taken care of. The phrase I remember hearing over and over again was, "Doc, am I going to live?" Telling these men that they would live was the only time I've ever felt that lying was justified, because I had to give them a sense of peace and hope.

We evacuated the wounded to the ships that were docked and after the beach was secure, we went back to our ship to take care of them. The hours were long as there were so many to be cared for and many surgeries were ordered. Men losing limbs was not a pleasant sight to see, and when they found out that the surgery had cost them the loss of their arm or leg, this was heart-wrenching.

Not only did the war cause emotional and mental harm, but it also took a toll on my body. Shortly after the attack, I was spending the day taking care of the wounded and went up on deck to take a break. I was having a cigarette when I heard a big gun go off near where I was standing. That explosion, as I found out later, destroyed half of my hearing.

After hearing machine guns, I looked up and saw hundreds of Japanese planes in the sky. They were called Kamikaze planes, Japanese pilots that had a one-man mission, which was to crash their plane into a ship and die with the plane. I was running to the sick bay where all the patients and medical staff were when I looked to my right and saw a Kamikaze pilot coming in low. I could see he had his focus on what he had to do. His target was the battleship *New Mexico* which is the second largest ship in the Navy Fleet next to the aircraft carrier. My job was to save lives, yet here was a young man giving up his life on purpose. He hit the bridge of the battleship *New Mexico* and killed eighty men, including the captain. The Japanese sent over 4,000 of their young men to die on those planes. Ten percent got through and hit over four hundred ships. We were fighting a very tough enemy.

The battle for Okinawa was one of the bloodiest of World War II. The Japanese lost over 44,000 soldiers; the United States lost over 14,000 men and our wounded were over 62,000. The Japanese had never lost a war, and the Kamikaze pilots were a daily affair we had to deal with. The enemy pilots mounted additional bombs to the planes to cause more damage; however, the extra weight slowed the planes down, which gave our gunners a better target to hit.

After the battle, we took the wounded back to Hawaii to recover or be sent home. We were there for about two weeks so we could have some shore leave and try to enjoy Hawaii. It was good to have some normal life to help us temporarily forget what we had gone through, but soon we had to go back to sea. We loaded lots of supplies and a large contingent of Army men. We knew something big was going to happen. The word was out that we might be going to invade Japan since we had taken over Okinawa. We went out to sea and joined a large group of miscellaneous ships. We knew it was going to be a big invasion. As we got closer to Japan, we got news that we had just dropped an atomic bomb on Hiroshima. We heard that it killed and maimed thousands of people, and later we heard that they dropped another bomb on Nagasaki that also killed a large amount of people.

A few days later we heard that the Japanese surrendered and the war was over. We were so happy and figured that we would turn around and go back to Pearl Harbor in Hawaii, but they told us to go into our assigned invasion spot which was the Naval Base in Sasebo, Japan. We had to enter Sasebo through a waterway bordered on both sides with hills and caves. The Japanese had gun emplacements in the caves, and if President Truman had not made the decision to drop the two atomic bombs, we would have lost thousands and thousands of men on the ground. Going into that inner harbor would have made us like sitting ducks in the water.

I have felt regret that many Japanese people died from those bombings, but, on the other hand, millions of productive people lived and had children that grew up to become very productive citizens. Much of the technology we enjoy today was developed by the Japanese. If the war had continued, a lot of those inventive, creative people could have died or never been born. Consider the two Japanese men that founded the Sony Corporation, or Daisuke Matsushita who founded the Matsushita Company, which later became Panasonic. If the war had continued, perhaps they might have been killed or some other aspect of the war may have hindered them from moving forward with their businesses. Our world, technologically and in other ways, could have been very different if the war had continued on.

We did not encounter any fire or other big problems when we entered Japan; in fact, the Japanese were waving to us as we came in. We set up camp somewhere in Sasebo and were there for almost a month. We got weekend passes and went to town to buy items and have a few drinks.

The people were nice to us, but also very cautious. When we would go into town, we found that we could buy things very inexpensively. For example, one of my shipmates bought a beautiful tea set which included six cups and six saucers for only 25 cents. Jewelry boxes ranged from 10-15 cents, jewelry was 50 cents to one dollar, and most food items were around a nickel. Enlisted men were given only three dollars in Japanese money for spending, which was enough to buy a lot of items because things were so inexpensive. Americans who were not aware of this would often overpay for an item. In one instance, this mistake ended up raising the prices on everything for everyone. My comrades and I were in a store buying something when an officer came in and saw an item he wanted and said to the clerk, "I will give you one dollar for that item" when he could have gotten for 35 cents. Because he overpaid, within a few weeks everything was double the price. We caused our own inflation.

Our occupation of Sasebo came to an end for our outfit after almost a month. We received orders to go back to Pearl Harbor and then back to the United States mainland. Our ship, the *Bowie*, came back to pick us up along with another big Army outfit. This time it appeared my journey was taking a turn for the better, and I felt less fear and anxiety as we crossed the Pacific Ocean.

We were at sea for many days heading back to Pearl Harbor in Hawaii. On board we took care of any sick, assisted in surgeries, and completed other medical tasks. I assisted in at least ten appendectomy operations and I really felt confident after all that time that in an emergency I could take out a guy's appendix. It was a great experience and made me want to become a doctor. I sure had come a long way from that seventeen-year-old that could not stand the sight of blood.

We arrived in Hawaii, refueled, took on more troops, and then sailed on to the United States mainland, headed to San Pedro, California. When we arrived at San Pedro, we were told we were to unload the troops, refuel, take on more supplies, and then leave in five days. I had a weekend pass and went to Los Angeles.

When I got back, I found out that we were sailing to some place in the Pacific. We were to leave in the morning and be gone for three months. It was now the beginning of December. I was up on deck and went by the Yeoman's office to check the Navy bulletin which was always posted outside of his office so we could catch up on the latest news. I saw a notice that if you had thirty-one points (we were given more points for being overseas), you could be discharged, unless you had signed up for the regular Navy service term, which was four years. I had only signed up for the duration of the war, and on this day, I discovered I had thirty-three points awarded to me. I notified the Chief Yeoman about this, and he contacted the captain of the ship. The captain told the Yeoman to get my papers ready and get me off the ship before they were to sail in the morning.

My buddies helped me pack my duffle bag, we said our goodbyes, and they put me on the captain's small boat, on which I went to the San Pedro Naval Yard. They did not know what to do with me since it was evening, so they gave me a twenty-four hour pass and some money to go to Los Angeles, which was about a half hour away.

I had a great time in Los Angeles, staying at a nice hotel and exploring new venues, feeling like a free man. I returned to the Navy Base the next day late in the afternoon. They gave me my discharge papers and more money. They also gave me a train ticket to New York where my family was. They asked me if I was wounded while I was in the Navy. I wanted to tell them that I lost half my hearing and was having horrible flashbacks related to the past trauma I had been through in the service, but I figured they would keep me there longer which would delay my return to New York. All I wanted was to be home for my twentieth birthday, which was December 19, and also to celebrate Christmas with my family.

HOME AND ALIVE

I arrived in New York two days before my twentieth birthday. I had joined the Navy at seventeen years old, weighing 135 pounds, and I came home weighing 170 pounds, mostly muscle. My family nearly fell over when I knocked on the door and, boy, did we have a great party that night. It was amazing to see the people I loved most in the world and to spend Christmas at home with them. My heart felt so full of joy to be back, but the war had changed me, and I wasn't the same man that left home. The flashbacks of the war were consuming me. Seeing the Kamikaze planes that took so many lives by diving into Naval ships. Thousands of our young men killed and wounded and watching them die on the beaches and in my arms. I still can't remove those images and they continued to come back over and over again. I was suffering from Post Traumatic Stress Disorder, although I didn't know it. What had the war done to me?

After being home for about a month, I decided to further my education. Since I had been in the medical corps and had all that experience, I decided I wanted to go to school to become a doctor. There were a few credits I had to procure prior to going to college, and after that was completed, I could start my pursuit towards applying for medical school.

I found a high school further downtown from where I lived to take a required Algebra class. I sat in the front of the class, and being a comedian, I was always telling jokes when class was not in session. After a few weeks, I found out a guy who sat next to me quit school, maybe it was because of my jokes.

There was an empty seat now next to me, and a beautiful girl with exotic brown eyes, asked me if the seat was open. She said she could see and hear better if she were closer to the front. I later found out that she asked to sit next to me because she thought I was cute. She was the smartest girl in the class, so I figured that if I needed help, I had the right answers available in the form of this lovely woman. I soon found out how wrong my thinking was. It turned out there was no way she would allow me to cheat on the exams using her answers, and Mary Jo made me figure it out on my own. That was an eye opener. What a woman of integrity (as well as many other qualities) she was!

I found out that she lived five blocks from where I lived, and we began to ride the subways together to and from class. It didn't take long for me to fall in love with this smart and beautiful woman. Eight months later I asked her to marry me, and she said, "Yes."

I was twenty years old and she was just a young seventeen. We figured if we asked our families about getting married, they would say that we are too young. Therefore, we decided to run off and get married in New Jersey, which was just across the river. My best friend Gabe became my best man. My wife to be, Mary Jo Velazquez, chose her best friend Effie to be the maid of honor.

We got our license in Union City, New Jersey, and

got married in a small Lutheran church across the street in Weehawken, New Jersey, by a Reverend Fegley. It was on a Sunday afternoon on June 22, 1947, which happened to be Mary Jo's eighteenth birthday.

We congratulated each other, said goodbye to Gabe and Effie, and went to my mother's house where we always had a big Sunday dinner. Every Sunday at my parents' home was a family day with relatives gathering together. Since I was staying with my parents at this time, my new wife and I went to my house.

Mary Jo and I arrived at my house around four o'clock. My mom and dad were getting dinner ready for the family. My grandmother had come over for dinner as well. No one in my family or my new wife's family knew we had gotten married. But while we were eating, my grandmother said to my wife in a very thick Russian accent, "You look too happy today, like you got married." Mary Jo almost choked on her food. We all laughed and Jo said, "Oh, it's because it's my birthday."

It was always wonderful to have my grandmother and her feisty spirit around. My grandmother, Paulina, was a very wise woman that emigrated to the United States from Russia. She lived in Russia with my grandfather, who was an opera singer, and she was a ballet dancer. When the Bolsheviks took over Russia, my grandfather being wealthy, had to get out of Russia. He took my grandmother and the four children (two boys and two girls) to Shanghai China for protection. At their expensive hotel was my father who worked as a clerk for reservations (he spoke seven languages). When he and my mother saw each other, that was it. Against my grandfather's rejection, they fell in love and got married. They moved and settled into New York City. Now back to my wedding day.

Later that evening I took my new wife to her home, kissed her good night, and went back to my parents' home. We finally told our families a week later that we had eloped. They were hurt, but my family loved and accepted Jo, and her family accepted me as well.

For a few months we lived with Jo's family until we found an apartment close by. Apartments were hard to get at that time. Our first apartment was shared with a woman who rented us the back part of the apartment she owned. We had to share the kitchen. The only problem was that she was an alcoholic, and many times we had to pick her up and put her to bed. Not a way to start married life. Eventually we got another, more private place.

I worked in a factory for a while, and then I learned a trade that my father taught me, which was hanging wallpaper. Dad and I worked very well together as a father and son duo, and bonding started taking place. It was a wonderful experience.

In spite of my new married bliss and spending so much quality time with my father, I was still having terrible flashbacks about the war. I was afraid if I said anything about what I was dealing with, that someone would think I was crazy and they would put me in a mental institution. I had worked in a mental ward in the Navy, and it scared the hell out of me. My own wife did not even realize what was happening to me, because I got so good at masking my pain. I filled my mind with humor and busied myself with many projects as a way to cope with all of the mental trauma.

I also medicated myself by drinking too much alcohol. We had never heard of Post-Traumatic Stress Disorder, and I never sought treatment until years later. I carried the burden of these flashbacks for sixty-six years because at that time I really didn't know what to do to cope with my pain. Since comedy had always been one of my "coping mechanisms" which helped ease the flashbacks, I thought that pursuing a career as a professional comedian might be a way to cope with all the trauma I was dealing with. I needed to catch a break and get my foot in that professional door.

Jo and I on our 25th Anniversary.. Renewing Vow

HERE COMES SHOW BUSINESS

One day, my Uncle Bill had come for a visit. He and his wife, Sarah, were in show business. They were successful dancers and worked in various nightclubs and theaters around the country. My uncle was also a very good opera singer, which added to his performance versatility. In addition, they added some comedy through jokes they included in their act. It was a good stage act.

While they were visiting, I was asked to tell a few jokes and do some impersonations of the actors that were popular at that time. I had the ability to do many dialects, such as Irish, Russian, Scottish, French, plus Jewish and Southern accents. My memory for jokes was like a computer, and that ability, along with my sense of humor, had all the makings of a successful comedian.

My Uncle Bill was impressed with my talent. He suggested that I work up a few comedy routines, and he would give me a spot in his show. I said that I would work on it and contact him within a month. When I was ready, I called him and told him about what I had prepared and performed some of it to him over the phone. He liked what I said and sent me and my wife money to come down to Jacksonville, Florida, where he

34

and my aunt were working at the time.

Jo and I decided to travel down to Florida and we found the nightclub to be very nice. There were two shows a night from Tuesday to Thursday and on Friday, Saturday, and Sunday we did three shows. On Mondays the club was closed, which gave us a day off. In the show, Bill introduced the female singer who performed three numbers, and then Bill and Sarah danced the Tango and other ballroom dances. Sarah had a single dance number followed by Bill coming out and singing a couple of songs. Later in the show, Bill introduced me as the comedian who had traveled all the way from his dressing room near the toilet to make us laugh. "Here's Jackie Walker," he'd say.

I have to admit, I was quite nervous doing my first professional show. The butterflies in my stomach were really flopping. I'll never forget my opening joke:

I was on a train coming to Florida, and I sat near two people that did not know each other. I overheard the man say, "Lady, I don't want you to think I am making a pass at you, but I see that diamond on your finger. That's the biggest diamond I ever saw." She replied, "Oh, this is the Clotman Diamond. It's like the Hope Diamond, but it comes with a curse," she explained. "What kind of curse comes with the Clotman Diamond?" She said, "MR CLOTMAN!"

The audience laughed out loud and, from then on, I was on a roll. My time slot was fifteen to twenty minutes, and I was a big hit with the crowds. My starting salary was $250 a week. Most people were making $50 a week on average. I had a wonderful wife and a good job doing what I loved, along with free room and board that the club paid for.

Entertaining was a part of my journey that I loved,

and I didn't want it to end. My Uncle Bill and I did very well together, and he decided that the comedy portion should be expanded by doing what we called "The Battle of Wits." We would bounce jokes and barbs off of each other. This routine went over very well with the audience.

I would sing a phrase in a comically bad way and Bill would ask me, "Have you taken singing lessons?" With a smile I would say, "Yes, I did, and it was very expensive." Bill would then say, "You should have talked to my cousin, Louie." I'd say, "Is he a singing teacher?" Bill would reply, "No, he's a lawyer, and he will get you your money back." Another time I said to Bill, "I went to the library and asked the clerk for a book called *Man: Master of Women*." Bill would reply, "What did she say?" And I would respond, "She said I'd find it in the fiction section."

We did the show successfully for a month and drew in the crowds. After that Bill wanted to strike out on his own and he didn't mind that the owner of the club asked me to stay on as the main act with a $500 a week salary to start. We parted as friends and I was very grateful to him for helping me get my start in show business.

I was known on stage as "Jackie Walker, The Man of Many Dialects." I did three shows a night and was very successful. The boss gave us a cabin near the club for free to reside in. I soon received a raise to $750 per week. I had over fifteen suits with shoes to match (we dressed up in those days). I was in my third month at the club, and was very popular. I also did a ten-minute spot for the Elks and received $100. It was a huge deal when most people were only earning around $50 a week back then. My agent contacted me and said he could book me into one of the biggest clubs in Charleston, South Carolina. The starting pay would be $750 a week, with a potential of earning more. It would be a big step up for me. He had seen me perform and liked my work.

I told my boss that I would give him two weeks notice before I would ever leave. He loved me and would always give me a hug and say, "You're my man." However, when I told him I was going to leave the club, he took me into his office, and then I found out who he really was. I had heard that the Mafia owned a lot of clubs all around the country, and this was one of them, along with the one in Charleston. I used to see his friends come into the club as his guests, and I believed they were wonderful and generous people. However, when things didn't go right, God knows what happened to those involved.

He sat me down, took a gun out of his pocket and laid it on the desk. He then proceeded to curse at me like I used to hear when I was in the Navy. Frankly, he scared the hell out of me. I was only twenty-one years old, and after he finished ranting and raving, I offered to stay until he found a good replacement for me. I told him I knew a guy who performed my style of comedy. He agreed to my terms as I also told him I would be back after the Charleston gig. I got the guy and he came to the club. The boss liked him and agreed that he would fill in until I came back.

Jo and I traveled to Charleston and I opened at a big, beautiful nightclub. It had large circular driveway from the road to the front door. It was about half the size of a football field, and it was shaped like a horseshoe. South Carolina was a dry state back then; no alcohol or gambling was legally permitted. The club had liquor and wine in pitchers instead of in their marked bottles.

Dealing with the police was a common occurrence. If the police raided the club, which usually happened twice a week, a man stationed at the door looking through a large peephole would alert the club. Since the driveway was half the size of a football field, there was ample time to dump wine and liquor down the drain before the police arrived at the club's front door. It didn't matter if the police smelled the liquor because they had to find the bottles to prosecute, which they never did. They were also not allowed to touch a customer's drink even if there was booze in it.

When it came to gambling at the dice table, everything was done using cash, no chips. There was a room near the bar with double doors on it. All of the gambling tables had wooden flaps attached to them. Whenever the police came, the man at the door would give a signal and a light with a buzzer would go off. Everyone took their money and the table flaps were lowered. A big cloth was thrown over the tables and drinks were set on it. The police were not allowed to check the tables. I often wondered if someone on the police force was paid off, so that when they would show up they never saw anything or prosecuted anyone.

I started to suspect this one night when my wife had an encounter with the police. Jo needed a job to do while I was performing shows, so I got her a job with the club being a "beat my shake" girl. Before you let your imagination run away with you, I will explain. A "beat my shake" girl had three dice. Gamblers made a bet with her that their roll of three dice would beat her roll of the dice. The bet could be in any amount from one dollar to whatever the club set as a limit.

Her "career" was short lived. On her first night, she had two hundred dollars in cash that the club had leant her. She was young and very beautiful. The police raided that night and my wife, running scared, took the cash and ran into the restroom. She was in the bathroom for over a half an hour. The police left after fifteen minutes, but before they left, the captain or the police picked up the dice that were on the table and gave them to the club owner and said, "Tell your 'beat my shake' girl to not be so nervous next time."

When Jo came out of the bathroom, the boss went over to tell her that it was okay. However, my wife gave him all the money and quit on the spot. There was no changing her mind, though there was debate over which was her worst option, listening to my jokes all the time or being a "beat my shake" girl. She chose the first option.

Our life at the club lasted over one month and was very interesting. The boss liked Jo and me, and he invited us to have lunch and go flying with him in his Navy plane. He took me up first, and we flew over the huge waters of the Cooper River. He buzzed the ship, did a few turns, and then headed back to the field. It was fun and exciting. Then he took Jo up and flew under the Cooper River bridge, which was against the law. My wife still talks about that flight, even after all these years. Our life there was like something out of a movie.

I did really well with my routines, bringing in the crowds. The press was good, which helped a lot. I did a routine called "Honey Suckle Rose." I sang in a style as if I was a gay man, and it was very well received by the audience at that time. My act would begin, "I wanted to get into the WAVES (the women's Navy). They said, "You can't get in!" and I'd say, "Why?" They'd say, "You're a man!" Then I'd say, "I have my mother's features." Followed by, "Yes, but you have your father's fixtures!" Well, everybody loved the routine.

I also had lots of high-class people that came to see my show. There was a woman, I'll call her Sue, who came to the club with a few friends and she always ordered two to three bottles of champagne, plus she ordered the wonderful sizzling steaks they served there. A few times Sue arrived with her girls and asked me to join them. We were talking and laughing when the owner of the club came over and told me that a really big name politician in the town had come to the club and he wanted me to cut out the "Honey Suckle Rose" number. He said it was too suggestive. Sue overheard my conversation with the owner and told him to go back and tell the politician that she liked that number, and she wanted me to continue to do it. The owner went back and told the politician what Sue had said. The politician then smiled at Sue, raised his glass, and whispered in the manager's ear. The manager came back and said, "The gentleman would be happy for Jackie Walker to do that number."

I asked Sue what she was holding over Mr. Politician's head and she said that he was one of her biggest customers. She then told me she ran a large house of prostitution. I must admit this was a part of my journey I hadn't envisioned, but it was intriguing.

One night my boss told me that some guys from New York were coming to the club to see me. They were in a new media called "television." I was very nervous knowing this and thoughts swirled in my head as I wondered what in the world "television" was.

That evening the television representatives arrived and there were two of them who I was introduced to. We briefly talked about their search for new talent for television. I had not seen television at that time, and it sounded strange to me. It was like movies only in your home. Sue was there that night, and I was sitting with her before the show. I normally did not drink before a show; however, I was so nervous with the television representatives being there that I had two glasses of champagne.

When I came out on the stage I got one joke out and then blanked on the next joke. Though I finally got my act going, I knew it wasn't my best performance. When I got to the table after the show to talk to the television reps, they said, "You were good, but you need to work on your act a little more." They gave me their card and told me to look them up in six months. Because I knew it was the champagne that messed me up, from then on I would never drink in between shows.

I continued working at the club and loved the people. I was held over at the Charleston club for another two weeks. I experienced the seedy side of life as well as the good side. I met many wonderful people while I was on the road, but my wife wanted to have children and for us to settle down into a more normal family life. I agreed to do weekend performances around New York and in the Catskills where they had lots of resorts. However, the agents could only do so much in getting bookings for me unless I was willing to travel. Because we were going to start having children and traveling would be difficult with a family, my wife and I decided that I would get a regular job, residing in one location to raise our family. Once in a while a local gig came up, and I would take it to earn a few extra bucks, but that was the extent of any show business endeavors now that a family with children was on the horizon.

I would like to pause here to tell you that I was not a Christian at this time. I went through the war without knowing God in a personal way. I lived the crazy wild life of show business. Prostitutes and gamblers were my best friends. One night in between shows, a man from the band came to my table while I was having coffee. He said, (after some small talk)He told me about his life and how he found Jesus. Then he said "Jackie, do you know Jesus?" Now men in the band are wild guys! I said, "Yes, I have heard of him." He then asked, "Would you like to accept him as your savior?" I answered, "No," and he asked me why. I then told him that I have some sins that I am enjoying and I don't want to give them up. He went on to say, "Why don't you ask Jesus

41

to come into your life, but tell him you don't want to give up those sins. If he does not want you to have them, let him take them away." It was a challenge to me, and I decided to do exactly what he said. I took Jesus as my savior. After that experience I started to clean up my act and my life was starting to change. I was ready to take on an average job and become a father.

Jack Doing Jimmy Durante.

BIG CAREER CHANGE

I applied for a job with the Singer Sewing Machine Company in Manhattan, New York, since I lived close. It was then that I made my move from show biz to the sew biz (forgive the pun). Having been a professional comedian and having a love for people, I became a salesman. They taught us the basics about how the sewing machine worked so we could demonstrate them. We would get calls from people who were having trouble with their old machines and we would have our mechanics check them out. While we were servicing their machine, we would leave them one of our new Singer machines. We demonstrated all the new and unique features, including the zigzag stitch and how to embroider your name on a shirt or blouse. It was like leaving a puppy with a child for a week and then trying to take it back after they had grown to love it.

The estimate we gave them on their old machine was always a little higher, due to something we missed. We would tell them the repair cost for their old machine and then present a way for them to keep the new machine. We would offer money for their old machine, an affordable monthly payment, and free service calls. We sold a lot of sewing machines using this sales

43

method, although I'll admit it was slightly manipulative.

We also had a great vacuum cleaner that could become flat and you could hang it on a door or wall with a nail. We would bring the vacuum with us as we demonstrated the new sewing machine or worked on their old machine and would purposely throw the threads or small items on the floor, so we would have an excuse to use the vacuum. While cleaning up, we would show them the new features of the vacuum and make price comparisons with our competitors. Our price was always the lowest one, but despite our cunning sales techniques, we still rarely sold a vacuum.

Salesmen like myself were given a company truck to carry extra sewing machines and vacuum cleaners in. When writing the contract, if we sensed a hesitancy in them giving us their information, we would obtain it shrewdly by mentioning that they might not qualify, but with a few pieces of information, we could check and find out for sure. This provided us with their occupation, length of time on the job, address, phone number, etc. Then we would tell them their application for a new sewing machine could be submitted with a ten-dollar deposit of cash or check. This all contributed to bringing about the sale.

I was successful as a salesman because I had a product I believed in, which is vitally important. I didn't want to cheat people out of their hard-earned money, so I made sure, through asking questions, that the item I was selling would be beneficial for them. My concern for my customers helped increase my sales. Unfortunately, I had a sales manager that was tactless with the sales force.

At meetings, he would embarrass a salesperson and use foul language. It got to the point that I couldn't stand him and wanted to leave my job. At that time, my father, mother, younger sister, and brother decided to move to California. Since I was not happy with my boss, my wife and I decided that our family would move there, too. By this point we had two children and a third due any day. Our oldest was our daughter named Lesley and she was around four years old at this time. Her sister, my daughter, Paula, was eighteen months younger. Our son (to be named Craig) was due any day. Adjusting to being a father was a new challenge for me, which I gladly took on. It was a challenge for Jo as well, since she was a first-time mother. To my knowledge, there weren't any parenting classes at that time, so we did the best we could.

By now you may have guessed that I did not pursue becoming a doctor. My mindset then was that I had a lot of responsibilities and no time or money to pursue medical school. Looking back on my life's journey, I still have ended up touching lives, but in a different way than if I had become a doctor.

I asked for a transfer to the Singer Sewing Machine office in Los Angeles and they granted my request. Before I left for California, I told the sales manager that I believed he was one of the worst motivators for salesmen that I had ever known. He did not like what I said, but there was nothing he could do to me, since I was going to be leaving for California. I didn't care about the fact that he could have tried to notify the Singer Company in Los Angeles that I had a bad attitude toward management. I believe this was one of my ways of subconsciously sabotaging myself.

The owner of the moving company who was taking our furniture and personal belongings across country had a brother-in-law who was a manager for a big drug store chain in California. He told me that if I didn't like my job with the Singer Corporation in California to see his brother-in-law. I decided to keep that suggestion in the back of my mind, just in case.

As we prepared for our journey, I discovered that my

good friend Danny had a pretty decent car and was thinking of moving to California as well. We worked out a deal that we would split the gas and hotel expenses, except that I would pay extra for my two daughters' meals, as they would be accompanying us. Since my wife and new son couldn't go by car with us, we arranged that they would fly out to California and meet us after we arrived and got settled with the girls.

The drive across country with two little girls and two men was a nightmare. We had no idea how to take care of little girls, except for making sure they were cleaned and fed. Tasks like fixing their hair, etc., were foreign to us. Thank God we made it safely and the girls survived, despite our ineptitude.

My wife and son arrived in California a week after we had gotten there with the girls. Our first priority after arriving was to find an apartment to rent. We found an apartment with an extra room for Danny to occupy until he got his own place.

With our housing situation all taken care of, I began my job with Singer. It was going fine, about the same as it had been in New York. I had been working for the company for about three months in California when I decided to check out the big drug store chain that the mover had told me about. I went to their main office and introduced myself to the personnel manager. He gave me some written tests, interviewed me, and then he introduced me to the manager in charge of all the drug stores. He was a very nice guy who I remember had an excellent memory. His first question was regarding what I expected from his company. I told him that I expected them to allow me the freedom to be creative and work hard which would make them more successful. I felt that if the company was more successful through my efforts, then I, in turn, would end up more successful. I was hired on the spot to become a manager trainee. To get that position with the large drug store chain was a big deal to me, and I was excited.

I began working for the drug store chain two weeks later, after giving Singer notice. When I met the manager of the store, Morris, he had a cigarette dangling from his lips. He was a very nice man and took time to show me the different departments in the store and how much profit each department made. I found out rather quickly that the pharmacy was the most profitable department of all. After showing me around, we went to the fountain to get a cup of coffee. At that time this drug store chain had what was like a mini coffee shop within the store.

I worked hard to provide for my family. I was known for my tenacity and competitive spirit. An example of that tenacious spirit was related to a conversation I had with Morris. We were talking about the business, and I asked him how long, on average, did it take for someone to become a manager. He said that it took around five years. I looked at him and said, "I will make it in three years." He gave me a condescending smile and said, "Good luck."

During the time I was involved with all my career pursuits and managing the drug store, my children were growing up. I later realized I was so busy with my career that my children seemingly had no father to love, discipline, and spend time with them. At that time I was very happy with Jo raising our three children, while I worked hard outside the home earning the money to support my family and achieve some form of success. But this career approach caused me to end up neglecting my family. I now believe that in trying to eliminate those awful flashbacks from the war, I was keeping myself busy with work. I was sabotaging the most important things in my life. Oh, sure, I gave them material things, but I did not give of myself and my time. I didn't spend time with the kids playing, nor did we do things together as a family. In fact, I hardly saw my family, because my work hours were always late into the evening.

One day on my day off, my daughter Lesley who was five, did something wrong. I gave her a whack on the butt. She did not cry, but instead put her hands on her hips and said, "When did you become the boss in the family?" I looked at my wife and she calmly said, "You're never here to be a father." That shocked the hell out of me.

After that I told my boss that I had to have more time with my family. He agreed, and I reworked my schedule so I could spend more time with them. I set up a plan to take each of my three children to the pancake house every Saturday. Each child had that one-on-one time with me and, I will say, it was a blessing. They also looked forward to those times together. I found out a lot about my children through these meetings. When you spend time with your children, ask questions and eliminate the short version answers like "ok, yes, ah huh." Ask questions that make them give you long answers or share a recent story that happen to them. Then, and only then you start to bond with your children.

We began planning family vacations and other family functions. I had promised to spend more time with my family, and I kept my word. This is so important to children. Too many times we think that if we break our word, they will get over it and forget the incident, but that's not usually the case. Everything is magnified to a child, and breaking your word to them is not easily forgotten.

I enjoyed having my immediate family and relatives on both sides of our family in California. We all grew to be a tight-knit group and would show a lot of affection when we'd have family social events. We were a hugging, kissing family, and it did not matter who was around, because that was the European way families greeted each other. We continued that tradition with all of our family.

From Los Angeles we moved to the city of Norwalk, and started attending a small church in which our family became active members. With my experience in show business, I participated in various activities there that utilized my talents. For example, I did Biblically-related shows where I participated in musicals they produced.

During our time there, my wife became pregnant with our fourth child. When it came time for the delivery, the child passed away. Outside of the war, his death hit me the hardest in regards to traumatic experiences in my life. I thought that God was angry with me for my past transgressions, but a pastor talked with me and told me that God's ways were not like our ways. He went on to say that some day I'd know the reason why we lost our child, whom we had named Eric. I accepted the pastor's explanation, and went on with my life.

A little over a year later my wife became pregnant with our fifth child. It was a baby girl that she carried to term and delivered, we named her Dana. But that baby girl only lived a few days and also passed away. My wife lost a lot of blood with this delivery, and at one point we were not sure whether she would survive.

Though neither my wife nor I understood the reasons behind our children's deaths, my wife was more open to trusting God than I was and put all the pain in his hands. As for me, I became very angry with God because I truly believed he was punishing me for things I had done in the past. Because of this type of thinking and my anger towards God regarding the babies' deaths, I was contemplating not going to church anymore. But I was well-known in our small church and knew that they would come to my house to find out what was wrong if I stopped going.

My negative feelings towards God, along with my

flashbacks from the war, were driving me to do many crazy things. I will not go into all the details regarding what a man will do when he is desperate and grieving, but it's not a pretty picture, and one I am not proud of. I treated my wife badly. She did not deserve that kind of treatment, and I have often asked myself, why did you sabotage your marriage? While I was dealing with my flashbacks and grief and turning away from God, my wife was continuing to grow in her faith. To me, we were heading in opposite directions.

Later in life, I would learn some of the reasons why I behaved this way, which included subconsciously not feeling worthy of being loved. Because of that type of thinking and subsequent behavior, it was a miracle my wife didn't leave me. Thankfully, she stayed.

I learned that in life, we often think that the grass is greener on the other side, but those who go to the other side find that it usually isn't greener, but only appears that way. I have found that if you water and culture your own "grass" with tender loving care, then over a period of time, you will see how much greener your grass will become. It took a number of years before that truth became a reality in my life. As the years rolled by I have found that marriage is not a fifty-fifty proposition. You must give more than that to make a marriage work. I always tell people if you want more love, than you have to make the bigger effort. I give the example of seeing your spouse as a cup. Fill that cup full of love, and all that overflows is yours. Take time to appreciate the little as well as the big things you do for each other. It took a while, but with God's help, we have a great romance going.

MY UPWARD CLIMB

I worked hard in many different facets of the drug store business, especially in the area of sales promotions. For example, I built beautiful displays and sent them to the home office to see what they thought. They liked them and ended up using them throughout the drug store chain. Another example of an idea that I had at that time was when I went by the department where they sold watches, and when I asked the sales clerk the price of the watch, she had to lift it up and look underneath to get that information. This method of sales took more time and consequently, more money, so I decided to make up a plastic tag with a price on the top of the case instead of underneath. This way, the customer could see the price without having to ask the sales clerk for assistance. We doubled our sales of watches. I sent that idea to the home office, and they thought it was a good idea and used it in a slightly modified version. They used plastic price tags that went into the metal clips that snapped on to the front of the glass shelves. This way, a perspective buyer could see the prices more easily. Through my hard work and some innovative ideas, I got to be well-known.

Within two and a half years, I went from third

assistant to assistant manager and eventually I was made a manager. I spent nine years in that position and had lots of interesting experiences. A few of them I will relate in the pages ahead.

One interesting experience that comes to mind was one that happened during the busy Christmas season. We hired detectives to catch shoplifters. I hired one who I will call Stewart. He was a detective with the Los Angeles Police Department. He worked weekends for us and was good at picking out the shoplifters. A man came into the store and he walked around looking at items and picked up an expensive pair of sunglasses. Stewart saw him put them in his pocket. As the man went through the front of the store, his girlfriend spotted Stewart and gave a sign to the man that took the glasses. There was a stack of cookies on top of the ice cream counter and as the man turned to leave, he flipped the glasses on top of the cookies. Stewart did not see the man put the glasses there, so he caught him outside and brought him back in. The man started making a big fuss to attract attention and I was watched Stewart ask him to take everything out of his pockets. The man complied, but there was nothing there, and I could see a potential lawsuit unfolding. The man yelled out loud, "You thought I stole something!" Stewart said, "Who said you stole anything?" He took a picture out of his pocket of a man and quickly showed it to the crowd and said, "You look like this man."

As he showed the picture to the crowd he told them that the man was wanted for murder. The shoplifter screamed, "I ain't no murderer! I swear I did not kill anybody!" Stewart said, "I don't know if what you're saying is true or not, but I will give you the benefit of the doubt. Get your butt out of here!" The guy ran out. Afterwards I told Steward what a clever move that was and asked how he thought of it. He said,

"I was as shocked as you were, but I thought I would give it a try." Later on we found the glasses on the cookie display. Stewart was well worth the money we paid him.

Another big incident I encountered as manager involved hiring a new employee for my store. A man came in asking for a job and I will call him Mac. I needed a man to stock the shelves and mop the floor each night. I gave him the application papers to fill out and bring back. He returned the next day with all the papers except the fingerprint form. He said he had to get that from the police station (which we paid for), so I put him to work stocking and helping to mop the floors three times a week. He did a great job of stocking and doing anything that was asked of him, and I really liked the guy. A week went by and the main office asked about the fingerprints on Mac. He kept making excuses and said that he would get them. Many nights it was him and I that closed the store, and I would have him take the nightly receipts to the safe, which contained lots of money.

One night when we got ready to close the store, I asked him if he wanted to have something to eat. We were both hungry, so we went to an all-night restaurant. Mac seemed to be a nice man who had lived a hard life, which could be seen in his face. Through many great conversations with Mac, I got to understand him much better.

I was looking for a special case of liquor that I had ordered for a customer, and found it had disappeared. I asked the liquor clerk if he had sold it or had any idea where it might be. I then reported it to our security department and they said they would keep a watch over our store with a stake out.

My regular man along with Mac were stocking the shelves and cleaning the floors. By the back door there was a big box of shiny striped paper, the kind they used for packing. They asked me if they could take it home so they could use the shiny paper for an upcoming party. I checked the box and it had just the paper. When they got ready to go, they had to call me to open the door.

My "late girl" employee and I were counting the money and recording it. When I opened the back door and Mac picked up the box with the shiny paper, I noticed his muscles ripple, which told me the box was not just shiny paper strips. Knowing that there was a stake out, I let them go. Ten minutes later there was a tapping on the glass door. A man showed me his badge and, after opening the door, he proceeded to tell me that he and his partner were taking the box and the two men to police headquarters. There were other policemen there at the time as well. They told me to stay at the store until they came back. Two and a half hours later one of them came back and told me the men had been arrested for stealing.

The security man from the company gave me a list of the items being held and said they would be returned at a later date. He asked me how the two men being held were hired and why their fingerprints were never taken. I told him that Mac would keep making excuses and, since he was a good worker, I never pushed the matter any further. I told him that Mac and I worked and closed the store together many nights. The security man informed me that they ran his fingerprints and Mac was wanted on two counts of murder. My stomach churned! The security man went on to say that Mac stated that he wasn't sorry for anything, except he felt bad about "disappointing Mr. Gutman." He said that I was the only man that treated him like a friend. I whispered to myself, "Thank God." I do not know what happened to Mac, but the other man that worked for us got one year in jail.

Things went well for over six months. I found out that I was being considered for a promotion to district manager, which would give me a nice raise. If I got the promotion, I would oversee ten stores in my district. Was I about to embark on a new, rewarding path on this journey I was on? At the moment, it was looking promising.

A few weeks went by, and one evening one of my good customers came in. He had two prescriptions that he purchased every thirty days. One item was a drug to pep you up and also suppress your appetite, while the other was a type of insulin. He said that he had run out and needed it right away. The pharmacist had left for the evening, so my customer said he would bring the new prescription in the following afternoon. He always got the prescription and was a good customer, so in good faith I gave it to him and left a note for the pharmacist about the transaction and the prescription being brought in the following afternoon. I found out that the customer did not have a new prescription and had lied to me. Of course, the pharmacist had to call the head office and report it.

Two days later, I was called into the head office. At that time I had been with the company for nine years. I was well-known and about to be promoted. In fact, I had thought that was why I was being called into the head office. When I walked into the big boss's office, there was the personnel manager and two security men present. They asked me about the incident with the prescription item that I gave to the customer and I told them the whole story. I figured they would tell me not to do that anymore. They told me that they had been very happy with my work and that they liked me a lot, but that I should not have given that man the prescription because I was not the pharmacist. I explained that he had been purchasing that item for over a year which they understood, but I had broken corporate rules. I was then given the choice of either resigning or they would have to fire me. What a blow! I thought I was going to pass out. Nine years was down the drain because of this one incident. Knowing that I could have a cleaner record by resigning, I took that option. I felt so embarrassed and humiliated. The company and I agreed to put on my record that stress was the reason for leaving.

I was given a severance check and told the pension that I had accumulated with the company would be sent to me. We shook hands and they said they were sorry it had turned out the way it did. I had to go back to my store and get my personal things. I was accompanied by a security man. They counted my cash box and took my security codes. I told everyone that I was resigning due to stress. There was a lot of crying and sadness with my crew. My heart was breaking! The worst part of all was that I now had to tell my wife what happened. This took a terrible toll on me. I became depressed and did a lot of drinking. This new issue, along with the flashbacks was almost more than I could bear. I again sabotaged myself when everything was going so well. God in his word (the Bible) says: "No test or temptation that comes your way is beyond the course of what others have had to face. All you need to remember is that God will never let you down; He will never let you be pushed past your limit. He will always be there to help you come through it" (I Cor. 10:13 MSG).

I read that Scripture over and over, but it eased the pain only a little. The loss of my managerial position, along with my flashbacks from the war, was causing me to move to more self-destructive ways of behavior in my life. A few months later we were hit with a lot of bills I didn't have money to pay. I was starting to feel desperate. I always thought the money would come in due to my promotions, so I over-extended myself.

One of the crazy thoughts I had to get out of debt was to rob a store. I had borrowed a gun from a friend, picked out a store, and watched the store's closing habits. Here I was, a Christian, planning a robbery. I had chosen the night I was going to do the robbery and I was determined I was going to do it, no matter what the consequences. God in the Bible says, "There is nothing that can happen to you that has not happened to others. However, if you trust me, I will not let you suffer more than you can stand. I will find a way to help you." I wasn't into the Bible that much then, so I wasn't familiar with that Scripture at that particular time in my life and my faith was not where it is now. It appeared nothing would deter me from my plan to rob this store, or so it seemed. It is amazing how your mind can justify stupid actions. In looking back, I realize now that I was a Christian in name only and only found out years later what true Christianity means.

Three days before the planned robbery, someone broke my daughter's watch. I told her I would take it to a store that was down where we used to live. I went there the next day, and the store was closed until 10:00 a.m. Angrily I pulled out of the driveway to make a right turn, but a car cut me off, and I ended up having to make a left turn. When I proceeded, I heard a horn honking behind me so I stopped. It was Don, my college friend, who was a strong Christian. He asked me to go and have a cup of coffee with him, and so I did.

In our conversation, I told him about my problems and plan to rob the store. He did not react in a judgmental, critical manner. Instead, he went on to tell me about some of the consequences of my actions if I got caught. I never gave that any thought when I planned the robbery. He mentioned what it would do to my family, to my church, and how God would feel. He also told me to pray about it. I left Don and decided to postpone it for a short time, but I still planned to go through with it at a later date.

That Sunday I went to church to make my weekly appearance, as I was well-known there. It was as if someone knew what I was planning and told the pastor about it because his message was aimed right at me. He ended by telling the congregation that they needed to come back to Christ. I was thinking that he couldn't have been talking to me, but then he went on to say, "Someone has fallen away from God and needs to come back." You can imagine the looks of the congregation when I went walking up that aisle. What I heard in my head was the Scripture: "Seek ye first the kingdom of God and his righteousness, and all other things will be added unto you." (Matthew 6.33)

At that moment I rededicated my life to Christ with tears in my eyes. My wife, who was growing in her Christian faith, was surprised but grateful for what had taken place. That night we prayed together and truly made God a priority in our lives. I no longer thought of robbing a store to get needed money. Instead, I was putting things in God's hands and trying to trust him to provide. This new walk with God was also a journey down life's pathway that still had its "bumps in the road." It was not "smooth sailing," but one where I still would stumble and fall at times.

Now that I'm much older, looking back on this incident, I can see God's loving hand of protection working in my life. Even when I was in rebellion, he still showed he loved and cared about me by having me run into Don, who in love pointed out consequences I never thought about. I thank God for his love, grace, mercy, and protection. He is a faithful God.

God made it clear to me in many ways that he was

merciful and loved me more than I could comprehend. He also made it clear to me and my family that he was our provider, and I didn't have to rob a store to provide for my family. God would do it, if I would trust him to do it.

A few weeks went by and a friend of mine from my church worked for Prudential Insurance Company as a manager. He heard that I had left my job and asked me to lunch. He offered me a job in the insurance business with his company and said he would train me. He felt with my sales background I would be a natural in the insurance business.

I joined the Prudential Insurance Company around October. Over that month, I went through training and studying for my license. I was given a salary plus commission. I was told that people did not buy insurance during Thanksgiving and Christmas. Being a go-getter, I went out and sold over a half a million dollars worth of insurance during that time. I learned a valuable lesson through that experience; to be careful about listening and acting on what others tell you to be true or tell you the way a situation always is. It has been proven that you will believe what you say more than what anyone else may tell you. Plus, the Bible says that, "As a man thinks in his heart, so is he." So what we think and say is very powerful in affecting what happens to us in our lives. Selling so much insurance during a period of months when I was told that can't happen is a good example of these principles in action.

I became very successful in the insurance business, and it helped my depression. I won trips and cash awards from the company by setting goals and achieving them. I found my name in various newspapers that mentioned my accomplishments. In fact, at one point I got a call from the boss at Occidental Life Insurance Company inviting me to his office and offering me a job as brokerage manager. The salary and over-rides were good, so I decided to take the job offer and gave the Prudential Company two weeks' notice.

I was with Occidental Life Insurance for over a year and did very well. I remember the company gave me a beautiful red Bonneville car for my use. It seemed I was taking another positive step in my life's journey.

Outside of work, all my involvement in the community was helpful for increasing my business. I had become a member of Rotary International, through which I made many good contacts for business. It was a respectable organization that I enjoyed being a part of. I also became a member of the Anaheim Chamber of Commerce, where I eventually became elected to Chairman of the Ambassadors. With my background of being a comedian, I did shows for them and was Master of Ceremonies for many of their events. I was in the newspaper several times because of the activities I participated in. One highlight was giving Nolan Ryan, a renowned, accomplished baseball player of that era, an award from the pitcher's mound at Angels stadium in Anaheim, California. I told a joke to the audience at the time of presentation which fortunately went well and got a lot of laughs.

As Chairman, another perk was that I had was the privilege of meeting various celebrities and movie stars. I worked on the committee that arranged the Bob Hope Charity for one of the big hospitals in Anaheim, California. Bob Hope came with a whole band plus a few girls that sang, and the event was a great success. He was truly a great humanitarian.

Later in 1979, I was contacted by the manager of Travelers Insurance Company. They had read about me and some of the things that I had accomplished. I honestly believed that I did not accomplish more than other agents did but just happened to get more publicity because of my associations, comedic performances, etc. I was called into the office and offered a great job as an insurance agent with Travelers. They offered me a nice starting salary until I reached that amount with my commissions. They were also willing to help pay for my license to sell mutual funds and certain bonds. This gave me a lot more earning potential. The kicker was that they would help me get my license to sell casualty insurance, which included selling homeowners and auto insurance. It was a deal that I couldn't turn down. I talked to my manager at Occidental about my offer from Travelers, and he agreed it was a good deal. I gave three weeks' notice so I could help train a new brokerage manager. I left Occidental on very good terms.

My training with Travelers was long and hard, but worth it in the end. I had to study for both the security and casualty licenses. Plus, I had to learn all the policy types Travelers had. They put no pressure on me and gave me plenty of time to learn. It paid off, and after six months of selling I was doing well and passed the salary they had initially given me. They also gave bonuses which provided me with a very nice income.

At the end of my first year, I had written over $1,000,000 of whole life insurance policies. I was named "Rookie of the Year" of the West Coast for Travelers and was chosen to go back to Philadelphia to spend two weeks with the top twenty agents in the country. We were treated very well and they taught us new techniques in selling business insurance. Something that I always remember about that time was a particular restaurant experience. Travelers took us to a fancy restaurant while in Philadelphia. Though there were twenty of the top insurance agents in the country there, the waiter took all the cocktail, regular orders, and deserts, plus the other beverage orders without writing any of them down. He never made a mistake, either. I realized you can have the least important job on the planet, but if you can give your job an interesting twist, you can be successful. That waiter had people lining up to have him wait on them because of the interesting twist he gave to his job. I learned if you think outside the box, success with await you.

When I returned from Philadelphia, I worked very hard with long hours. After two and a half years with Travelers, I felt that I was getting very stressed out. The company was very good to me, but wanted me to keep producing. One day I was called into the office, and I had a nice conversation with the top executives of the company. They wanted me to set a goal to double my insurance sales production. They would give me bonuses, and provide me a private secretary and a corner office with a big glass window to enjoy the view. Was this finally the start of my best years? Well, it was sure looking more like it was. I worked hard for seven months, but I found the work was not fun anymore. I would end my days exhausted! I was giving great thought to making a change in my career.

NEW ADVENTURES

While I was with Travelers Insurance, I did some comedy shows and I also acted in some plays at Melodyland Christian Center. It was a big church I attended located in Anaheim, California, and they produced theater-type productions two or three times a year. Though I didn't sing, I was pretty good at the acting.

Since Melodyland Church was originally a theater in the round seating about 3,500 people, it was very conducive to theater-type productions. I also did four plays and a movie for a Christian group outside of Melodyland. The movie I acted in for them was called, *The Duke of Earl*. I played an alcoholic father that disliked his daughter hanging around a Mexican gang. It won a Dove award, which was similar to an Oscar or Emmy, except they were given to acknowledge Christian entertainment endeavors.

I was introduced to Pat Boone, a popular singer and actor, who started performing back in the 1960's. An actor and Christian friend of Pat's had seen me perform some comedy routines and told Pat about me. Pat wrote me and said that he needed a comedian to work with him and his wife and four daughters up in the San Francisco Bay area. He arranged for us to meet and discuss this possibility at Knott's Berry Farm in Buena Park, California, where he was doing a show with his family. We talked and worked out a deal for me to perform with them.

Not too long after that, I met him and the family at a hotel near San Francisco. We did a show at San Quentin prison, which was in that vicinity. Despite tight security, the show went very well. Pat and Shirley Boone plus the four daughters were a big hit. In my part of the program, because of the incarceration situation, I had to use jokes that were not related to wives or family. After the show, one prisoner told me I had made him laugh and I thanked him for that. I asked the guard what he was in for, and the guard told me it was for murder. Performing there was quite an experience for me.

Our next performance was at the Circle Star Theatre in San Carlos, California, for 3,000 people. Though this theater was in its prime at the time we performed there, it no longer exists. It was a unique theater in the round, featuring a rotating and circular stage with none of the 3,743 seats further than fifty feet from the stage. You stood on the stage in one spot and the stage moved around very slowly so you got to see all the people as you were performing. Another very unique experience.

We were going through a rehearsal one afternoon before our performance that night, and the sound and lights were going crazy. I was back in my dressing room resting and I got up and started talking to Pat. I said, "Pat, how can you stay so calm when things go wrong?" Pat looked at me and said, "Jack, outside I am calm, and inside I am asleep." In other words, he just stayed calm inside and out.

The show went very well, but we had to get back to Los Angeles because Pat had a commitment he had to fulfill. The traffic was terrible when we were driving back to the airport, so Pat said, "Let's pray." One of the main things we prayed was about making it to the plane on time. Those prayers got answered and the freeway opened like the Red Sea. We made it to the airport and got on the plane in time. I looked at Pat and said, "I can't believe we made it." Pat looked at me and said, "Well, didn't we pray about it?" That taught me a very valuable lesson about the power of prayer and praying in faith, believing that what you're praying about can happen.

We arrived back in Los Angeles, and I said goodbye to Pat and his family. The man that I had filled in for was coming back from vacation, so it looked like my time working with Pat was coming to an end. Though he had said we would work together again, it never came to fruition. I enjoyed working with a real professional and a gentleman, which he was. Also, his family exemplified a Christian attitude and I liked that. His daughters had different careers and challenges in life, (in fact his daughter, Debbie Boone, had a big hit record entitled "You Light Up My Life"). She went on many programs on television and also sang for one of our Presidents. The whole family stayed close to God and were great Christian examples to other people. I'm grateful to God for the opportunity to work with this wonderful Christian family.

I went back to Travelers and my regular job of selling insurance. About a month later, I got a call from the owner of a big insurance brokerage house. He had heard about me and wanted me to have lunch with him. He said it would be worth my while.

The owner of the firm, I will call him Bill, showed me a great health plan that gave you a million dollars coverage. At that time hospital rooms were under $50 a day to stay, and his premiums for this plan were fantastic. If I told you the premium, you would not believe me as you are reading this today. He had the exclusive right to sell this plan here in California. That got my attention. The next thing he showed me was a whole life insurance plan that would give a person double the insurance that a "twenty pay" life insurance plan normally gave. Plus it gave the person the same cash value at the end of twenty years. A "twenty pay" plan means you pay a certain monthly premium based on how much insurance you had wanted to purchase. At the end of the twenty years you got back almost all your money. The premiums were almost the same as other plans that didn't give that type of return.

All of this intrigued me, but I still wasn't sure I wanted to make the move and work for him. I told him that I had a nice office and a private secretary where I was now. He promised me secretarial help, but it wouldn't be private. I told him that I had a car given to me to use with my present company. He told me he would get me a car for my personal use, and the company would pay for it. Now when it came to commissions on auto, health, commercial, and mutual funds, he guaranteed me a draw on my commissions at a high rate. If it did not exceed my commissions, I would not have to pay it back, which was a great deal. I told him that I had to sell my accounts with Travelers and it would take three weeks to one month to make the change. He agreed to my terms.

I gave my notice to Travelers, and they tried to talk me out of leaving. The pressure they put on me regarding doubling my goals was another sign that I was ready to leave. I also felt that the new company would give me a fresh start. It took close to three weeks to conclude my business with Travelers, but I was excited to begin a new journey.

I joined the new company after a week's rest. Using the techniques Bill had shown me, I started writing a lot of health plans and selling mutual funds, but the large commission came from the insurance sales, at which I was very successful. At first Bill did all that he had promised me, but after two years, he started to cut back on what he had promised. I finally decided that I had had enough of the insurance business, so I sold my accounts and decided to go into retail selling. There was a man that I bowled with who owned a big adhesive company. I told him that I was going to leave the insurance business. He asked me if I would be willing to work in his company and eventually become the sales manager. The salary and commission he offered was great, so I accepted. Another career move for me.

I went to work for him about a month later. There were accounts I had with my previous company that were sold at half their value. I did this because I was tired of the insurance business and wanted out, but as I look back, it was not one of the wiser decisions I made in my lifetime. That's because the accounts I sold held for many years, and they gave the agent who bought them lots of residual commissions. However, I don't want to dwell on the past because it could drive me crazy. This was another way residual effect of the PTSD. I sabotaged my business, where I could have received double the amount for those accounts, but I turned over to him. Looking back, I just did not care, and I kept doing stupid things subconsciously, believing that I did not deserve success.

STICKY BUSINESS

Getting into the adhesive business was an interesting experience. I had to learn a lot about it because I knew very little when I started. There were so many different types of adhesives and the materials they would work with.

One of the accounts I had was the company Bondo, which made materials to repair the metal on the fenders of a car. We made a few adhesives that would work with their products. To further my education in adhesives, I agreed to take an adhesives course twice a week at USC in Los Angeles, California, which the company paid for.

I worked during the day, and twice a week I took evening classes. Interesting enough, I would have dinner in the USC cafeteria before my class and would often see O.J. Simpson eating with friends in the cafeteria at that time. For those who have never heard of O.J. Simpson, he was a star USC football player who was accused of murdering his wife and her friend. Though not convicted of that crime, years later he ended up in prison for another crime he was convicted of.

I finished the course in adhesives, receiving a

certificate acknowledging my accomplishments. I was building my territory for the company with a goal that when I hit a certain amount in sales I would get an additional 15 percent on all monies over that goal. I received an order from a company that I had been working on for over a year. It was a huge amount and it would give me a commission on that order alone of $2,500, but the order had to be shipped out during that quarter to qualify. My boss, who I thought was my friend, dragged out the order delivery over a three-month period so the amount of the commission would overlap into the next quarter. Dragging it out like that minimized my commission as you had to hit a sales limit each quarter. Then I got another big sale, and he cut my territory in half, which also lowered my total sales. I asked him why he had done this to me, and he said that he had to distribute the territory so it would be fair to the other salesmen. I told him to give me that company as it is in the middle of my territory. His reply was, "Oh, that's a company account."

A month later, he raised my quota an additional $10,000. The sales manager job after almost two years was put off for another two years (he said he was not doing it for a while to save money). It was obvious he wouldn't allow me to succeed, probably because he didn't want to pay the extra commissions, or maybe for some other reasons I wasn't fully aware of. I decided I had enough and left the company on not so friendly terms. I told my boss I thought he was my friend, but if this was the way he treated friends, I wondered what he did to his enemies. He didn't comment.

A short time after I left the company I was at a football game with my good friend Chuck, who was an attorney. He asked me about my job and why I had left the company. I told him what had transpired and he said, "You have a good case against that company." We sued him and he settled out of court. I received a nice settlement, part of which I used to take my wife to Bermuda and a few other places. Often we would raise our wine glasses and toast to the man who had tried to cheat me.

I had a neighbor that lived across the street from me that was president of a company that had home ocean oyster pearl parties. The way it worked was that you invited friends, relatives, and neighbors to your house for a pearl party. Guests could pick out one of the oysters to see what kind of pearl they would get that they could have mounted in some kind of jewelry setting the company provided for purchase. Every oyster had a pearl in it as they were inseminated with an irritant (in this case one made of plastic), which irritated the oyster. To protect itself, the oyster would cover the "uninvited visitor" with layers and layers of nacre until the pearl was formed. The "irritated" oysters were put in baskets in water for around a year and fed off of plankton in the water. Many factors affect the pearl's size and color, including factors like the species of pearl oyster, length of cultivating time, temperature of cultivating water and even the harvest season.

My friend told me about how his company was growing and that he was looking for a public relations man to visit various parties and travel across the country video taping some of those parties for training purposes. He offered me the job, and after mulling over his offer for a while, I decided to accept it.

The salary and office I had in Hollywood was very acceptable. I was also given a beautiful Cadillac for my traveling. I had to do some additional training at the Hollywood office on how the operation worked. I learned how you teach people to book parties and get your friends to book parties. You gave a nice piece of jewelry that the company had a pearl mounted on, to the hostess having the pearl party. The hostess was also givens 50 percent off any piece of jewelry the company had pictured in their catalogue.

At the party, when you picked out your oyster, it was then opened, cleaned and measured. Guests only paid three dollars for the oyster of their choice. Once chosen, the guest could choose a setting from the catalogue to have the pearl put into like a ring (the most expensive) or a pendant (the least expensive) and there was a setting for every budget. The parties were a lot of fun, and the value you got was worth the price you paid for the item.

I was recently in San Francisco at Pier 39 and saw a stand that sold the oysters and pearls. They were doing the same thing we had done. The only change was that the oyster you bought was not three dollars but was now fourteen dollars. I guess inflation has hit everywhere, even with the oysters.

I was asked to go across the country and videotape some of the various parties. I was trained on how to use the big video camera with a tripod. We did not have the nice small video cameras like they have today. One of my main duties was interviewing the host or hostess that had become successful in this business. We called them jewelers. Most people when they are in front of a camera or audience of any type freeze up. That was one of the reasons they hired me. They had seen me do shows and talk to people and knew I could make the people feel at ease.

We would set up appointments with the various jewelers connected with the company. I would arrive with all my equipment, and establish a friendly atmosphere with the jeweler. I would set up the camera and sit across from them. The camera was operated by a remote control that I had in my hand. I would set up the lights, and then we would be ready to begin. A majority of the time the jeweler would become stiff as a board with fright. To relax them, I drew on my comedic past and told a few jokes. Then I would ask them about their family and let them discuss comfortable topics. When I knew that they were more relaxed, I clicked on my remote and began filming which they were unaware of. I asked questions about how they became so successful and business techniques. The jeweler would then start telling me their story, for example, how they needed extra money, and then they tried the pearl parties. I would then ask another question like how they got new customers and new jewelers under them. After a while you couldn't stop them from talking. Because they didn't realize we had already been filming, they would often ask when the filming would start. I would then tell them that it was already over. The look of surprise on some of their faces was priceless. Though they didn't say so, I think they were not just surprised, but I think they were also relieved that it was already done. When I sent the videos back to my office in Hollywood, they could not believe the relaxed quality of the jewelers. I told them what I did to calm the jewelers down and they loved it!

On one of my business trips, I was going all the way to New York so I decided to bring my wife so she could visit her family there. She flew to New York, while I drove there because of the interviews I had to do. We visited with her family for three days, then Jo and I drove back to California, interviewing some successful jewelers on the way back. The interviews went well, and it was a successful trip.

I created a spoof video of the business, showing how to have a pearl party. We did everything opposite to what the company wanted and the jeweler, who was in a t-shirt instead of a suit, and had rings on every finger, ended up being very successful. The DVD got lots of laughs, and the company said it was way before it's time. My son, Craig, performed in the video as a hippy jeweler. The interesting thing about the videotaping was that I was in every one of the scenes in some capacity. Subconsciously, I must have thought that since I was in every scene, I was locked in with the company, and they would never let me go. I eventually found that not to be true.

Six months later I was busy with the job doing shows for the company and also writing articles about various jewelers, when problems surfaced. They were having an unforeseen financial crisis and had expanded too quickly. Consequently, they had to cut staff. Well guess who got laid off just before Christmas? You guessed it, Jack Gutman, the public relations man. They gave me a nice severance package and let me keep the Cadillac for two months. In my opinion they were a good company to work for, despite their financial problems and having to let me go. At this point, it looked like my journey had hit a pothole in the road.

FROM JEWELRY TO COSMETICS

A good friend that I knew from the drug store chain I worked for told me about this company that dealt in cosmetics. He said they were looking for a salesman. I called the owner and he met me for an interview. He was a broker for various cosmetic companies, and he handled at least 30 drug stores and beauty salons. He needed someone to take over an established sales territory. I accepted and he gave me a nice salary, commission, and a car. It looked like a good job with a promising future, so I was now ready to learn the cosmetics business.

One of the cologne lines we represented was Jovan, a company with good products and a great reputation, along with other big-name companies. There was always a new item that came in that we had to persuade the store to try. Some store managers were tough to sell to, while others were easy. At this time, I was still getting the PTSD flashbacks, so learning the new business was beneficial for me and helped lessen them.

I was with the company for six months and doing well. The boss was actively involved in the business and held meetings with us at his home. He would expect us to not only spend a full day in the field doing sales, but also wanted us to do our reports and stay for a meeting he would put on. It seemed like we were always working around two hours over the eight-hour work limit, which had us putting in an average of ten-hour days.

I told my boss that I had a family and needed to spend more time with them. I told him I couldn't continue putting in ten-hour days, especially without any overtime pay. The other salesmen were single, so working many overtime hours didn't affect them the same way it did my family and me. Compromising, I said I would give two days of the work week at ten hours per day, but wouldn't stay the extra hours on the other three days of the week. He didn't particularly like that idea, but agreed to it.

He then started to cut back on the commissions that were promised. I don't understand the thinking of a boss that gets greedy and does dishonest things like mine did. It causes good employees to leave, and loyalty is so important to a company. If a boss treats his employees with respect, he will find that they will work harder. Some of the big companies today are doing just that and are very successful.

After the experiences with this particular boss and all the other many jobs and bosses I had in my past, I decided that I was going to go to work for myself as a wallpaper contractor. No bosses, no long hours, no playing by anyone else's rules, just my own. Since I wanted to build up my new business somewhat before I quit my present job, I stayed on for a while. We were coming to a holiday where we would be off with pay. I told my wife I was going to resign and she suggested I work through the holiday so I could get the extra pay. I had my paperhanging business ready to go at this point and had work set up for two weeks, but I decided to heed my wife's suggestion and work through the holiday.

When I reported to work after the holiday, before I could resign my boss and his assistant told me they were laying me off because things were tight financially. They gave me two weeks severance pay. Needless to say, I was a happy man. I could now be my own boss and set my own hours. I built up my business and one of the biggest wallpaper companies in the country stated in a magazine that I was "one of the top paperhangers in Orange County." That article helped bring in a lot of extra business so I added another male employee who was very good in wallpapering. I taught him some of the techniques I used, and he soon became my partner. Jim Lambert became a great paperhanger and a good friend. He later took over my business when I retired.

During the time I was the owner of the company, Paper Hangers Deluxe, we hired eight more men for our work force. We always had enough work coming in, so they never missed a paycheck. Because their work reflected on Jim, myself, and the company, they had to be top notch. I personally checked their work to be sure it represented the high standards and excellent reputation we had earned. On occasion, if one of them messed up their work, I redid it at my expense. I worked with my crew for sixteen years, and never took advantage of them.

When the wallpapering business slowed down, I was forced to cut down on my work crew. Workers' Compensation payments and other costs were draining me of any profit. I wrote to the Governor of California about it, and three months later they raised the rate a few dollars per payroll. I should have kept my mouth shut and never written, because it only ended up making things worse. Another thing that slowed down the wallpaper hanging business was that faux painting had become the rage. Many people found faux painting saved them money and gave a great new look to their home décor. I decided it was time to retire from the wallpaper hanging business.

The drinking problem was still going on, but it seemed to me it was in a "manageable" state. Then it gradually started to escalate. In the meantime, I was away from God and doing other things not right in God's eyes. But when you have flashbacks of the war almost every night for so many years, the loss of two children that I never got over, losing the managerial position with the drug store chain, lending money to people that disappeared and never paid back, it seemed too much for a human to handle on their own. Instead of turning to God, the only one who could truly help me, I turned to the bottle.

Consequently, life became hell. I would not drink while I was working, as my late father had programmed me to never work with alcohol in my system. However, when I got home, I would start drinking wine or beer at dinner. Then between seven and eleven o'clock in the evening, I would drink six more drinks. If anyone would ever try to tell me I was an alcoholic, I would get in their face and tell them that I never drank on the job. Also, at home, I knew my limit. Of course, before I hit my limit I was drunk.

I used to joke that a man was coming home staggering on the street. A policeman stopped him and asked where he was going. The drunk said, "I'm going to a lecture on alcoholism." "Who is giving the lecture?" asked the policeman. The drunk answered, "MY WIFE!"

All kidding aside, the drinking had a negative impact on my life in many ways. It was truly starting to get out of hand. For example, if we were invited to a party or dinner at a relative or a friend's house, I would not bring just one bottle of wine, but I would bring a half-gallon and many times, a whole gallon. Why? Because I wanted to be sure that I would not run out. Sometimes I would drive in that intoxicated state, and I am so fortunate that I did not get caught, or kill someone. I now realize how dangerous it was to drink and drive, and I'm very sorry for having done it. The most serious consequence of your behavior could be causing one or more deaths. Another consequence would be the costly fines. I hope and pray that anyone contemplating getting behind the wheel while intoxicated will think twice before causing some event that could alter their whole life or someone else's.

The drinking at home helped me sleep better and numbed the pain of flashbacks and other internal problems. However, my bottom (as it's called in AA) was a Thanksgiving Day at my son's house with the family. I had brought a gallon of wine and a magnum of champagne. The drinking began and I was having my fill. When Thanksgiving dinner was served, and all the family was at the table, I passed out with my face in my plate. What an embarrassment! When I found out what I had done, I cried. It was then I realized I needed help. My family (I found out later) had planned to do an intervention with me. Since my pride at that time would not have put up with that, it was better they decided to wait. Instead, my daughter Paula, who was a therapist, asked me to come to a special grief seminar that she was participating in which ran for many weeks. My wife went with me for support.

In the sessions, I found out the roots of my drinking problem. I also attended Alcoholics Anonymous, where I found a lot of men who were struggling with issues similar to mine. I received the most help from the Grief Recovery Institute my daughter Paula was involved with. Alcoholics Anonymous kept me on track, and I stopped drinking for over eighteen months. I am so grateful to Paula for her perseverance. Most of all, I am so grateful to my wife Jo for her support and tenacity to not give up on me and leave me during those difficult times.

I took a month off and enjoyed spending time with my wife. I also got to see my children who at this point were grown up, pursuing careers and living on their own. This time being off from work also allowed me to get some much-needed rest. Since my nature was to keep busy, I was still active with home projects and groups, such as the Christian Businessmen's Club. I spent many months with the Christian Business Men's Club doing what one of our Presidents named Dr Donald Smith called the Humor of Jack Gutman , I did 10 minutes of Jokes. Dr Don Smith was also an author and developed the video called the Silent Scream ! (about Abortion) He touched many lives During that time, I was at one of their meetings when a man whose name was Chuck Pennington approached me. He owned a successful used car dealership called Pennington Auto Sales for many years. Chuck asked me if I would like to sell cars for him. I told him that in all honesty I thought most used car dealers were crooks. He laughed and told me he tried to operate his business based on Christian principles. Since I had been good at sales, I decided to accept his offer.

I started to sell used cars for this reputable Christian car dealership. The majority of people would think that statement was a tongue-in-cheek remark, because of the negative reputation many used car dealerships have. I mean it from the bottom of my heart when I say that Chuck Pennington was a very ethical, knowledgeable, and generous man. It was a pleasure to work for him, though sometimes it can be difficult to know a used car's total history. Chuck did his best to know information and see that a customer got a decent car in proper working order.

During my first year with the dealership, I sold over a hundred cars and the second year around the same amount. I also used to help Chuck collect money owed to him by customers he had given credit to who were delinquent on their payments. Though the majority of people were very honest and fulfilled their obligations, there were a few that I had to use more creative methods to get them to make their payments. I found that humor could be useful in dealing with some of those types of accounts and people. For example, I would say, "You haven't made a payment for ten months. We've been carrying you longer than your mother." In most cases humor, understanding, and patience helped us avoid having to pick up their cars.

Chuck introduced me to Toastmasters International. I found them to be a great organization that helped me grow in the area of public speaking. I learned to speak well and became a motivational speaker. I won a big speech contest they had by telling an exaggerated story about one of my car test-drives with an English lady. It was a humorous presentation that helped win first prize. I highly recommend Toastmasters to anyone who deals with the public, especially in the area of speaking.

After two and a half years of selling used cars, I decided to sell new cars instead. I went to work for a big company selling many popular models. After some extensive training and learning about the competition, I was out selling new cars. I soon found out that the senior salesmen who were there the longest got most of the breaks and had their requests and needs taken care of before mine. An example of this was the day I sold my first car. I put in the credit papers for the department to process. It took over two hours for them to process what should have taken thirty minutes and my customers had to wait all that time.

I complained to the senior manager and told him that was not a good way to run a business. I also told him that I was promised I would get the full commission for the sale and that wasn't happening (they were giving half of the sales commission to the senior salesman that helped me close the sale). Because of having been in management in the past, I was able to spot a lot of inequities and brought this up to the manager. I was rocking the boat, and they didn't like it, so I was fired.

DESPERATE TIMES

As I was entering my eighty-fifth year of life, I found I did not have enough money for a decent retirement. I had made some bad financial deals in my lifetime and lost a lot of money. My savings account was slowly dwindling, and I was almost to the point of deep depression and hopelessness. For a man who normally approached life with an optimistic attitude, these feelings were extremely serious. I was not one who ever thought of taking his own life, but I knew that I had to do something to bring in some money for Jo and me to survive. I decided to put in an application with a big retail chain. I was not sure if they would hire me due to my age, but they did hire me, I think because of my past sales background and experience. I think having been a manager in a big drug store chain also helped my cause.

As I started this new job as a cashier, I reflected back on my life and felt my life was regressing. It seemed like I was at the bottom of the totem pole so to speak. I was also still facing flashbacks that just wouldn't leave me alone, which caused a lot of additional depression. I still hadn't told the doctors anything (because I was still thinking that they might lock me up in a mental institution if I told them the truth about what I was experiencing). Instead, I began busying myself with learning to be a good cashier. Believe me, there are so many things you have to know for various transactions, including knowing how not (to the best of your ability) make mistakes with money. I say that because there are unscrupulous people who use all kinds of tricks to try and get you confused, causing you to make mistakes at the register and I was an eighty-five-year-old man.

I felt a strong desire to try and touch lives while I was working at the register. I found that there were many lonely people who needed someone to talk to, care about them, and accept them as they were. I also felt they needed to trust God for their needs. Over my time working there, I spoke with many people. I would say to them, "How is life treating you?" I would get many different answers, but regardless of the answer, I would come back with, "I used to feel the same way. Then someone told me about trusting God. Though I took that step reluctantly at first, my life changed for the better. I felt, for my life, it was worth a try." I told them that what they did for their life was up to them. Many came back and thanked me, while others, I never heard from again.

Some employees of the company would come to me and talk about their problems. I would tell them what I would do in that situation. I received a great blessing by seeing lives changed. You run into so many lonely people every day, and all they want is for you to listen to them and show them you care. If you are in a situation where you are going to be sharing your thoughts on a matter, you might want to think and possibly pray about doing what I do. What I do is pray and ask God to give me the right words to speak. I know from experience He can and will do that.

At this point I have to skip ahead and tell you a story that relates to what I was talking about (I will come back to my cashiering days). My comedic background helped me get many side jobs of performing for different organizations. I was doing a fundraiser show for a church outside on their big lawn. The chairs were set up and people were waiting for the show. From somewhere in the audience I heard my name called. I looked and saw a woman with a baby, sitting by her husband. I went over to her to find out what she wanted. She wanted to know whether I worked at the place she had shopped at, which I told her that I had. She then went on to say that at that time she was pregnant and having all kinds of problems. She told me that I had talked and prayed with her. She said, "You changed my life!" One of the most touching things she said to me was, "You see that blue-eyed baby boy?" I said, "Yes, he's a beautiful baby." She said, "I named him 'Jack' after you." I have to admit I cried, because I was so touched. God had let me see once again someone whose life I had impacted and had a part in helping to change. You can do the same thing. Touching lives is a blessing that you can't put a price on. It's priceless! Plus, when you're helping others, your mind is off of yourself and your problems and focused on helping that person in need.

Now back to my cashiering days. I was at work as a cashier, and the scanner did not work. A customer came with her cart filled with many items. I had to pick each item up and scan it in front of the register. One item was a big bag of kitty litter. I had to go around and pick it up off the cart, and as I grabbed the bag and lifted it up, I felt something snap in my back. I reported it to the management, who in turn sent me to a medical facility. I had injured my spine and was in great pain. Although I hadn't been medically diagnosed yet, I was pretty sure that my cashiering days were over. After a year and a half of treatments, including acupuncture and electrostimulation, I was finally released from the company, still in a lot of pain. They worked out a settlement for me and I was released. I had to start living on Social Security and the money from the settlement. The money helped to take care of my bills, but without having a job to keep me busy, my flashbacks were coming back more often.

As time went on, I ran into family and friends that were having a rough time financially. I would write checks from $200 to $500 or even more as a love gift. I felt I was blessed, and they needed my help like I had needed years before. I kept giving without praying about whether I should give the money to that particular individual or not. Frankly, I wasn't using wisdom in my giving. When you have no extra income coming in outside of Social Security, your savings (which drew almost no interest from the banks) starts to dwindle.

After two years, we were broke again. I gave away a great deal of money, plus money loaned to friends that was never paid back. I found myself depressed and very unhappy. It is certain that this part of my journey was not a high point in my life. Jo and I ended up having to apply for food stamps (which was so humiliating). They started us with a monthly food stamp amount of $168 and we were so grateful for the assistance. We received that amount for a few months and then they lowered the assistance by half. They said the payment was lowered because our Social Security payments had a small "cost of living" increase that put us into a higher category. We just couldn't survive on such a small amount for groceries. We also had other bills we didn't have the money to pay. This difficult situation along with my flashbacks was causing me to sink into deeper depression.

POST-TRAUMATIC STRESS DISORDER

The Mayo Clinic defines Post-Traumatic Stress Disorder (PTSD) as a mental health condition that's triggered by a terrifying event, either experiencing it or witnessing it. Symptoms may include flashbacks, nightmares and severe anxiety, as well as uncontrollable thoughts about the event ("Post Traumatic Stress Disorder." Mayoclinic.org. Accessed October 26, 2015).

The Veterans Affairs Canada states "Memories and reminders of traumatic events are very unpleasant and usually lead to considerable distress. Therefore, people with PTSD often avoid situations, people, or events that may remind them of the trauma. They often try not to think about, or talk about, what happened, and attempt to cut themselves off from the painful feelings associated with the memories" ("Post-traumatic stress disorder and war-related stress." Accessed October 26, 2015. http://www.veterans.gc.ca). This description of PTSD and many of its accompanying symptoms listed above described me accurately.

At the time when the symptoms first started to appear in my life (post war experience), there was no such diagnosis. The flashbacks and the horrible things I saw and took part in were, to me, just bad memories. As previously stated, I thought that I would just have to live with it, and I also thought that if I told people or doctors what was happening to me because of the flashbacks, they would keep me under observation in some mental institution. What I had observed working in a mental health facility in the Navy for a month scared the hell out of me, so I kept my flashbacks and "demons" to myself.

There are several different definitions for the word "flashback," but the definition I use for the purposes of this book is from the Oxford Dictionary and states: "A disturbing sudden vivid memory of an event in the past, typically as a result of psychological trauma" (Oxforddictionaries.com. Accessed October 26, 2015. http://www.oxforddictionaries.com/definition/english/fla shback).

In my life, flashbacks were horrible things I had seen coming back to me in my thoughts and dreams. One flashback example I experienced was that of seeing two fellow Navy men get killed that slept near a road during one of our first practice invasions. They did not realize they were too close to the road where trucks and tanks came by. While they were dug in and asleep, a tank ran over them accidently. I want you to picture an eighteen-year-old coming to that scene and viewing those bodies, or any age for that matter being subjected to this type of trauma. It was so horrible to see. In your flashbacks the men screaming, "Mama, mama" are amplified, and you see it over and over again. Some of the other sights from the Normandy and Okinawa invasions are too graphic to describe herein, but this incident gives you an idea of what an impact witnessing a horrendous event like that can be.

In Okinawa, I remember the Japanese Kamikaze planes and young pilots, purposely killing themselves by piloting their bomb filled plane, into US war ships. There were over 4,000 of these Kamikaze planes, of which 10 percent got through and destroyed many American ships, killing many sailors. I'll never forget seeing the battleship *New Mexico* getting hit by one of those Kamikaze pilots. I could see the pilot alive for less than a minute, and then watched him crash into the bridge of the battleship. His vindictive act killed eighty people, including the captain of the ship. Since my job was to save lives, it was very hard to see men purposely give up their lives and end the lives of others in such a horrific manner.

The PTSD affected me not only with flashbacks, but took over me emotionally. When I went to see the movie *Saving Private Ryan*, which showed the Invasion of Normandy and the terrible bloody battle, I sat and cried for over an hour, reliving that terror. When I would watch a television news program that showed young men dying in various countries, I would remember the dead men that died on my watch on the ships and in the hospitals. I would recall the packing of every cavity in their body to prevent the leaking of body fluids. This procedure was very traumatizing for me, because those deceased soldiers were the same age that I was. Unless you have experienced it personally, you will never know the horror of it. Those flashback moments will fluctuate back and forth to the good times you had with your buddies, such as eating, drinking, and laughing about life, and then a few days later you're seeing their dead bodies. I often found myself questioning why they died and I was allowed to live.

I carried that and the other tragedies I had experienced for over sixty-six years. I would not talk about my war years, nor seek treatment for it. How did I cope? I covered up the pain related to the flashbacks and other bad memories, originally with alcohol, but also by using humor. Plus, I kept busy with other personal and family projects as well as working hard on my various jobs. These ways of "self medicating" were like putting a bandage over a bad wound and have it still bleed through.

I had been going to the Veterans' Administration for some other medical and dental assistance, and I finally told them about my flashbacks from the war. The doctor said I had Post Traumatic Stress Disorder (PTSD). I did not know what that term meant because when I was in World War II, that disorder didn't have an official name. I certainly didn't realize that it was a condition you could get help for without being thrown into a mental institution. The VA office received all my records together and set me up with a therapist to help me with this condition. My therapist was convinced that I had a problem and was willing to work with me to help me find relief. It was extremely challenging because our sessions would cause me to deal with my nightmarish war issues.

My first session with the therapist was a tough one. We talked and he got me to face the contents of some of those flashbacks. During these flashback episodes, I would find myself experiencing the invasions and other battle scenarios over and over again. I would hear and see the young men that were my age screaming for help. Do you know what it feels like when you hold a dying soldier in your arms, and he's crying "Mama, mama," and saying, "I don't want to die?" You lie to give him hope, and then watch him drift into death. In my flashbacks, I would see body parts on the beach and thought of them as someone's son, father, or husband that would never get to see his family again. I instantly realized that this could have been me.

When you are a medic, your relationship with the men you serve becomes very personal. It seems like the ones you save are your only salvation, but you're always haunted with the taunting thought, "Did I do enough or all I could?" When you are eighteen years old and in such a horrific war, you can only cope with so many traumas before it starts deeply affecting you in negative ways. Dylan Blender told me that I would eventually be able to talk about those things without the trauma.

After my first treatment with the therapist, I said, "The hell with it. I'm not coming back." I didn't want to relive those flashbacks any more than I was already, but I began thinking that I had already gone through sixty-six years of trying to deal with it all on my own through stuffing the feelings, covering them up with humor, and keeping very busy—none of which brought any lasting relief. I realized that all the things I had tried on my own were only masking the pain. So, after a lot of thought, I decided to go through with the treatments and started seeing the therapist regularly.

After almost two years of treatment and working through my flashbacks, I found that I could now talk about what I experienced in the war, the fears, and other memories, without falling apart or having to resort to the bottle. I realized that with the help I had gotten from the Veterans' Administration and God, I could live with the effects of war. God's presence in my life brought more strength and peace.

At the time of this writing, it's been almost three years that I've been in therapy with Dylan Bender. I can wholeheartedly say that going into therapy was one of the best decisions I've ever made and my therapist was a Godsend to me. To you veterans who are going through hell and trying to deal with it in your own futile ways, please take the opportunity to get help from the Veterans' Administration. Over time, you will hopefully gain freedom from the traumas and have some peace of mind. You won't regret it. I can't thank my therapist and the Veterans' Administration enough for providing us with doctors to help. To you veterans that are reading this book, please don't let the years go by without seeking treatment. We have lost too many comrades that

have committed suicide by not seeking help. I promise
you, there is hope and happiness ahead.

FINANCIAL DIASTER

The papers had been filed for my pension, and I learned I would see it approved and receive a check in a matter of a few weeks. I found out that this process can take a very long time, sometimes years, to be completed. Not only do all the medical records have to be gathered and reviewed, but many other factors are looked at as well. Plus, there's the fact of having to "wait your turn" because there are thousands of other veterans who are also applying for pension benefits.

In the meantime, my wife and I were still in need of financial assistance and not sure where to turn. We finally decided to approach our church, Eastside Christian, where we had attended for almost twenty-one years. They had a compassion program which helped its members and other people in the community who were in need. A friend of mine told me to talk to the people in charge of that program to see if they might be able to help us. I went there very reluctantly because I was ashamed of my circumstances. However, they were very understanding, and after listening to my situation, they agreed to pay our rent and additional bills for four months. They never made me feel inferior, but really showed love and understanding. I will never forget all the blessings given to us by Eastside Christian Church, and I found out that they had gifted around $5,000,000 to help people in need. So when you think all the church wants is your money, then talk to people like myself, who have had their lives blessed and quality of life improved through the love and help that we received from the church. They are not only helping people in our community, but are building structures, feeding and supporting people in places around the world.

We were told about food banks in the area, to which we also applied and received assistance. Any food we had left over, we donated to another church that always needed donations toward their ministry. It was a blessing to us that we were able to do that.

Though this was a very humbling time for my wife Jo and me, and it often looked like the pension would never be approved and all hope was gone, deep in our hearts we knew that somehow God would come through for us. We had been up and down that financial ladder many times, and now I was eighty-six years old. Because my life philosophy had become to touch lives in whatever way or with whatever talents God had given me, I continued that pursuit, despite my age or my financial situation. I did shows and also counseled with friends that wanted an ear to listen, or advice. I found joy in doing these things, but I was still in deep financial trouble. Though it often looked very scary, God always took care of us in some way and kept us going.

Another example of the blessings we received during that difficult time was my friend Steve Gonzales. Steve had been on a well-known radio station here in the Los Angeles area. He was a great radio personality and had also done some acting and modeling. He retired due to health issues. I would go from Anaheim, California, to Pasadena, California, to see him every two weeks and we would have breakfast together, talking about God and the lives we were living. He was always in good spirits. He knew my financial circumstances and always picked up the check, plus put gas in my car.

One day he called me and asked me to come to Pasadena for breakfast and prayer. I told Steve that I only had a quarter of a tank of gas in my car. He told me that he would fill my gas tank and buy me breakfast. So I went, and we had a wonderful time talking about God and life in general. Then when I was getting ready to leave, he gave me a twenty dollar bill. At that time I had only sixteen cents in my pocket, and God once again showed me his way of provision. Though this manner of provision may seem trivial to some, to me, it was a huge thing. On the way home, I had to pull over to the side of the road because I had started to cry. I was so tired of living on the poverty level, so I said to God, "I don't want to be a beggar anymore! I want to be a giver!"

At this time I also flashed back to the wonderful people God had used to help Jo and me when we were down and helped to keep us going through these difficult times. A majority of them have been named in the "Acknowledgements" pages of this book. I reflected on how God had used them all in different ways, to touch our lives through encouragement and financial assistance.

I remember I needed a minimum of $200 to pay a bill that was due. I went to our monthly meeting to have lunch and as I was getting ready to leave, Chuck Pennington stopped to ask me a question. After our conversation, I turned to leave, I felt his hand on my back and the other hand touched my back pocket. When I got to the car, I reached into my pocket and pulled out two hundred dollars that Chuck put there. I cried for ten minutes. This reflection helped me to also realize the faithfulness of God and that he would help us and not let us drown. Some of these same people also taught me that if you trust God and look to him, he would definitely take care of all your needs , I didn't realize how, in the days ahead, I would be having to trust God so greatly because of the ensuing challenges coming in regards to obtaining that pension.

I was frustrated when the Veterans' Administration contacted me and said that some information was missing that was necessary to help me qualify for a pension. They went on to tell me that with what they had in my file, they were not sure that I would qualify for PTSD. I angrily composed a letter to them, which said:

"Who are you to tell me that I may not qualify? I have carried those rotten nightmares of the men I saw die for 66 years, not to mention the screaming wounded crying, 'mama, mama!' with pleading eyes asking me, the medic, 'Doc, am I going to die?' Although I knew they would die, I lied and told them they would make it. Do you know what an 18- year-old feels when he sees a man his age lying there dead with his face blown off? Have you ever seen two young men accidentally run over by a tank? Do you know what that picture does to the mind of an 18- year-old kid?"

I showed this letter to my therapist. He made a copy and told me to visit a congressman or congresswoman to see if they could somehow help me. Half a block away was Congresswoman Loretta Sanchez's office. I went to see her and she read the letter. She told me they would help me. They sent their letter, along with mine, to the Veterans' Administration office. A few weeks later Congresswoman Loretta Sanchez and her assistant, Laura Martinez, contacted me and asked if I had heard anything yet. I told them I hadn't, and they told me they would follow up on the matter. Three days later the Veterans' Administration office said they found the papers they needed and were working on my case. Within three weeks I got the shock of my life.

I was having breakfast with my wife. We were eating

the cereal that we had gotten from the food bank. I was sitting depressed at age eighty-six, feeling that I would wind up dying penniless like my late dear father. It looked like my life's journey would bring me to a bitter end.

The telephone rang and a man identified himself as an employee of the Veterans' Administration. He told me that I had been approved for my pension for Post Traumatic Stress Disorder. The amount I would receive would take care of all our bills and a little left over. I was crying when I thanked him. He said, "Mr. Gutman, you have earned it." Then he said, "I am not finished yet, what is your bank number?" When he asked for personal financial information, my heart sank, thinking it was probably just a scam. Though there was only $25 in my account, I was still hesitant to give out personal financial information. The man then said, "Mr. Gutman, let me give you your bank number that you gave the veterans when you first filed. He gave me the number, and I said that was correct. He stated that the following Friday money would be deposited into our bank account. It was an amount I was not expecting and never thought could happen for us. With tears in my eyes, I thanked the man on the phone. After we hung up and I told my wife the figures, we both broke down crying and thanking God. Now it was starting to look like maybe my journey would not end in poverty and bitter despair, but instead, God's abundant provision and joyful hope would prevail.

As the days went on, I sent a letter of gratitude to Dylan Bender, who I was still seeing for treatment. I also sent a letter to Congresswoman Loretta Sanchez and Ms. Laura Martinez, thanking them for their fantastic efforts in getting my application expedited. Their assistance helped to give my wife and me a brand new life, for which I would be eternally grateful.

In the next two days we got off food stamps and notified the food bank we no longer needed their help. Because the food bank had been such a blessing to us during those difficult months, we now send them a monthly donation. We also reach out and help close friends that are in real need, although we don't go crazy like I did the first time.   Jesus said, "As you do it to the least of these my brethren, you do it as unto me." Of course, I also don't forget to give to Eastside Christian Church, who was a life preserver to a drowning man.

To you, the readers, especially you veterans, continue treatment for your specific problems. Seek various ways to solve your financial help. Above all, do not feel that there is no hope for you! If you believe that there is a God, then trust him. If you have not come to that conclusion, don't give up, God is always finding ways to reach you. Look at me, I went through two invasions not believing in a personal God. He gave me new life by bringing people into my life that have helped me get to this point. Whatever you do, DON'T GIVE UP!

CONCLUSION

Though my life's journey is not over, my journey thus far is nearing completion. In this concluding chapter, I would like to follow up on a few things and share some last words of advice.

Now how can principles in my life story be applied to your life? Though I have previously referred to this Bible verse, I am bringing it up again now because it helped me so much and may in the future help some of you. The Bible verse says, "There is no temptation taken you that is not common to man; but God will make a way of escape that you can bear it" (I Cor. 10:13). In other words, God will not let you suffer more than you can possibly stand, but he will make a way for you so that you can deal with it or be removed from it. Trust him, no matter how bad things look.

As I go into the winter of my life, I have learned a lot of things. Death is inevitable, and I know that like you, my days are numbered. What are you going to do with the rest of your life? I have decided to use mine to touch other lives in every way I can.

One of my last conversations with a dear friend before his passing said, "Jack, I love God and have accepted Jesus into my life and have tried to live a good life. But I wish I knew for sure what's on the other side of 'death's door?'" I said to him, "Karl, I heard a great explanation for death:

"There was a man visiting his friend at the man's house. They were sitting in his office. He said to the owner, 'What is on the other side of death's door?' The owner said, 'I don't really know.' The other man said, 'You are a Christian; you should know.' As the owner was ready to answer him, he heard a scratching on the door. The owner said, 'Do you hear that

97

scratching?' The man said, 'Yes.' 'The scratching is my dog. He does not know you are here, the only thing my dog knows is that his master is on the other side.'" I said, "Karl, when your time comes, your master will be waiting on the other side of death's door to embrace you." Karl thanked me with tears in his eyes and he died a week later.

I would be remiss if I did not update you regarding my wonderful family who has blessed my life over the years in so many ways. My wife, Jo, and I at the time of this writing, have been married for over sixty-eight years. Though there are some couples out there that have been married as long as we have or longer, we are all in the minority. Sadly, divorce is too prevalent in our society. I previously spoke about how we met and fell in love. Being married to me was not an easy task. Not only did I have a wild streak in me, but I put our marriage through hell because I was inadvertently sabotaging my life.

This sabotaging, I now know, was due to the PTSD. I could not accept the fact that my buddies died and I was still alive. This thinking was on a subconscious level, but transferred into my conscious behavior. Every time I achieved some success in my life or there was love or admiration shown towards me, I sabotaged it through some conscious action. Now with the help of God and counseling, the self-sabotaging has lessened greatly and I have been able to appreciate all the love and gifts in my life.

Lesley, my oldest daughter, helped me to become a better father. She grew up to go to college and pursue a career as a travel agent and also a musician, with voice as her major instrument. She graduated from college as a music education specialist and did a lot of solo singing for weddings, funerals, and banquets for groups like Rotary International, United Fund Organization, and others. She once sang on a UHF television station and performed a service on the radio that emanated from Catalina Island off the coast of Southern California. At one point in her career, she was able to have a professional CD produced of her singing.

Her singing career was cut short because she was diagnosed with Systemic Lupus, an auto-immune blood disorder in which a person's body tissues attacks its immune system, especially the vital organs, and this can be debilitating in many ways. Despite dealing with this disease, she has found many ways to touch lives through counseling and praying with people. Though she was married and divorced prior to being diagnosed with Lupus, she does not have a pity party as many people who go through a divorce and/or serious illness do, but she concentrates on her relationship with God and touching lives. She has been a blessing to me.

Paula, my second child, went to college and became a teacher. She taught school for a few years, and then decided to go into the movie business as a location manager. She worked with many big stars and had some good and challenging experiences in that business. Now a grief therapist, she has written several books and has a very successful practice.

Paula married and has two children named Erin and Casey. Erin is a talented woman who graduated from Chapman University in Orange, California, with a degree in the music field. She recently wrote a great book called *Party Girl—A Modern Fairy Tale,* which is a great read. Casey is a very bright young man who works in fine dining and has aspirations to work in entertainment and real estate. Paula's husband, Gary, was a producer on many television shows and worked with many big stars. Sadly, he passed away a few years ago from pneumonia.

Craig, my youngest graduated from college and developed a career in sales, spending over twenty years working with some well-known companies. He has been very successful in his career. I wish I had his computer skills because he is a whiz. He has been an amazing husband and father to his three children. Craig's wonderful wife, Marilyn, has a career in the educational field. She has been the strong, wonderful, wife and mother who helped, along with Craig, make their family successful. They have three children who are doing well in their pursuits.

Jenna, their only daughter, received her Master's Degree in Counseling. She presently works as a high school crisis counselor and also has her own private therapy office working with children and teens. Chris, their oldest son, is still going to college working on his Master's Degree, specializing in working with children with special needs. He recently was hired as a high school special education teacher. Their youngest son, Patrick, graduated with a Master's Degree in Piano Performance and Composition. He is currently a doctoral student at UCLA.

I am very proud of my family. As I reflect back on them, I realize that they're another reason why God protected me throughout the war. Had I not survived, none of them would be here, also touching lives the way they all are.

I refrained from drinking for a number of years. During those years, many things I learned helped me to deal with the roots of what made me drink. At the time of this writing, I am now able to have a glass of wine each evening. The tiger that AA talks about which is always thirsty for more alcohol has not awakened in me. It's been a few years like this of being able to have my glass of wine without abusing the alcohol. I have understood the reasons why I drank so much, and now I don't need to medicate myself with alcohol. You may ask the question, "If you don't need the alcohol to medicate pain anymore, why not stop drinking for good?" My answer is that I enjoy a good glass of wine once a day. Many who have been involved in alcoholism may disagree with me and think that you must stop drinking completely to maintain sobriety. I would not argue with you; I am only speaking for myself. For me, the various modalities that have been used to get me to this point of the healing I'm at now, allows me the freedom of having that daily glass of wine. Since many of the roots that caused me to use alcohol to medicate pain have been healed and my faith in God keeps growing, I feel that this daily glass of wine is all right for me. There was definitely a time when that would not have been the case. Each situation is different and must be decided on by the individual.

Now, how does my story relate to your life? We all have to go through various "wars." You name your "war." Is it stress related to your marriage, family, job, or drugs? Well, I do know that God has given each of you talents and various gifts. Use those God-given gifts to help other people.

Have you ever gone to apply for a job? The person interviewing you makes a decision to hire you and they go on to say, "If you do a good job during your trial period, we will keep you on permanently." God puts you on this earth and says to you, "While you're on this earth, use the best I have given you to help make life good for yourself and your fellow man." When you do something good to benefit another human being, your reward is very great in God's eyes. However, you cannot just do good works. God's word tells you how to find real happiness, joy and peace. I learned to trust and believe in what God said in the Bible, and it has changed my life greatly.

I have been on both sides of good and evil. I know that the dark side gives you lots of laughs and fun, but after a while, I had to admit that it was all vanity. Since I finally found God in my life (I am speaking only for myself), I have had much joy and peace of mind. I have a heavenly father that I can talk to daily. If your life so far has been miserable, maybe you can give God a chance.   Then, you will find joy, happiness, and peace. From that moment into eternity, you will know that your own personal journey was well worth it.

Family

Craig... Lesley...Jo...Paula... Jack

Cruise 2014 Jo and Jack

ABOUT THE AUTHOR

Jack Gutman is a World War II Veteran, comedian, and public speaker. He loves speaking to students and fellow Christians and touching lives with his story. He recently went to the World War II museum in New Orleans where they recorded his life story on video.

JackGutman.com

Made in the USA
San Bernardino, CA
02 March 2020